THE

WILD

COLORADO

*Fred Dellenbaugh in Lodore
Canyon on the Green River,
June 17, 1871.*

THE
WILD
COLORADO

The True Adventures

of Fred Dellenbaugh, Age 17,

on the

Second Powell Expedition into the

Grand Canyon

Richard Maurer

SCHOLASTIC INC.
New York Toronto London Auckland Sydney
Mexico City New Delhi Hong Kong

Quotation from Frederick S. Dellenbaugh's letter of June 16, 1871, by permission of
the Arizona Historical Society. Quotation from Frederick S. Dellenbaugh's diary
entries for July 26, 27, 31, and August 1, 1872, by permission of the Frederick Samuel
Dellenbaugh Papers, Manuscript and Archives Division, The New York Public Library,
Astor, Lenox and Tilden Foundations.

ISBN 0-439-18490-8

Copyright © 1999 by Richard Maurer. All rights reserved.
Published by Scholastic Inc., 555 Broadway, New York, NY 10012,
by arrangement with Random House Children's Books, a division of
Random House, Inc. SCHOLASTIC and associated logos are trademarks
and/or registered trademarks of Scholastic Inc.

12 11 10 9 8 7 6 5 4 3 2 1   0 1 2 3 4 5/0

Printed in the U.S.A.   23

First Scholastic printing, February 2000

Front cover: Artist Thomas Moran points into the Grand Canyon while
a newspaper reporter takes notes. Photo by Jack Hillers, August 1873.
(National Archives)

Back cover: The first detailed map of the Grand Canyon region,
based on the hand-drawn map of 1873 by Fred Dellenbaugh.
(Dellenbaugh, A Canyon Voyage, 1908)

Other picture credits follow the index.

To my sisters, Ginger and Rachel

Fred Dellenbaugh out west, 1872.

Contents

*Construction of the
Transcontinental Railroad at
the Green River crossing in
Wyoming, 1868.*

CHAPTER I
Looking for Adventure

May–June 1869

Fred Dellenbaugh had a lot on his mind as the summer of 1869 approached. Winter had been unusually long, even for Buffalo, New York. But by early May, as spring began to get a glorious foothold, the enterprising red-haired boy could turn his thoughts to life's impending great adventure: summer vacation.

Fifteen-year-old Fred would not finish his first year of high school until late June, but there was still plenty to excite the senses and feed the imagination until then. Speed demons were already taking to the streets and sidewalks on velocipedes, a type of bicycle with pedals attached to the front wheel. One citizen called them "the biggest nuisances in town." Soon swimmers would be diving off Buffalo's banks along Lake Erie and the Niagara River, and rowers would venture into the calmer stretches of the powerful current. Downstream the resorts at Niagara Falls were preparing to open, and school groups and families would soon be making the day trip to America's most famous natural wonder. Maybe this year a daredevil would walk a tightrope above the falls, as in summers past. Such stunts were considered foolhardy by many foreign visitors, but Americans prided themselves on having the freedom to try anything.

At the end of May there would be the solemn ceremony of Decoration Day, when Fred and his schoolmates would present bouquets of flowers for the graves of Union soldiers killed in the Civil War, just ended four years ago. Thousands were expected for this annual memorial, which was a somber contrast to the gaiety that saw the first Buffalo troops off to war in 1861. Fred at age eight had been there, wishing he were a drummer boy marching to battle.

As for vacation, he could hardly hope to top last summer's adventure

THE
WILD
COLORADO

when he rode the steamer *Fountain City* on a thousand-mile excursion from Buffalo to Chicago to visit his older sister, Sarah, and her husband, William, in America's most prosperous new city. Travel was in his blood now, and if he couldn't have more of it, he at least wanted to write about it. With a change of scene and a swashbuckling cast of characters, he believed his *Fountain City* experiences could make a terrific story for a boys' magazine, and he planned to work on it over the summer. There was inspiration aplenty at the library across from the offices shared by his father and uncle, Samuel and Frederick Dellenbaugh, both physicians.

Indeed, it was hard to stay out of the library, where he could always read the daily newspaper. That spring the papers were full of progress reports on the Transcontinental Railroad, being built east from California and west from Nebraska, and due to join any day in northern Utah to complete the first coast-to-coast railroad. The route had been under construction for more than four years. It would shorten what had once been a journey of many weeks into just a few days. There were also other stirring stories from out west—of gold and silver strikes, desperadoes, shootouts, and Indian attacks. One article was headlined HOW IT FEELS TO BE SCALPED: WHAT A VICTIM SAYS ABOUT IT.

In the same building with the library was an art gallery where Fred could fire his imagination with exotic landscapes. Drawing was another skill he intended to perfect over the summer, and although Niagara Falls was nearby he was far more attracted to the scenery of the West. According to the paintings he had seen, the region was filled with rugged snowcapped mountains and dark precipitous chasms. It seemed a magical place.

Fred spent hours poring over one book in particular. It recounted the experiences of Lieutenant Joseph Christmas Ives of the U.S. Topographical Engineers, who in 1858 led an expedition up the mouth of the most mysterious of all the great rivers of North America: the Colorado. Explorers knew of the Colorado's lower reaches, where it emerged from the desert into the Gulf of California. At its other end, they suspected it

was fed by the Green and Grand rivers, originating high in the central Rocky Mountains. But in between they knew very little at all, except that the Colorado ran through a remarkable gorge called by some Big Canyon and by others Grand Canyon.

Traveling by steamboat and rowboat, Ives and his party had made about 500 miles—from the Gulf of California, into the desert, through increasingly rough terrain and dangerous rapids—before abandoning the river and heading overland. They reached the rim of Big Canyon and climbed to the bottom, where they reconnected with the Colorado but saw no practical way to continue its exploration.

Fred was curious about the Colorado even before he found this book. On a school map he had plotted a route from the opposite direction—

The Ives Expedition, 1858. The beginnings of the canyons.

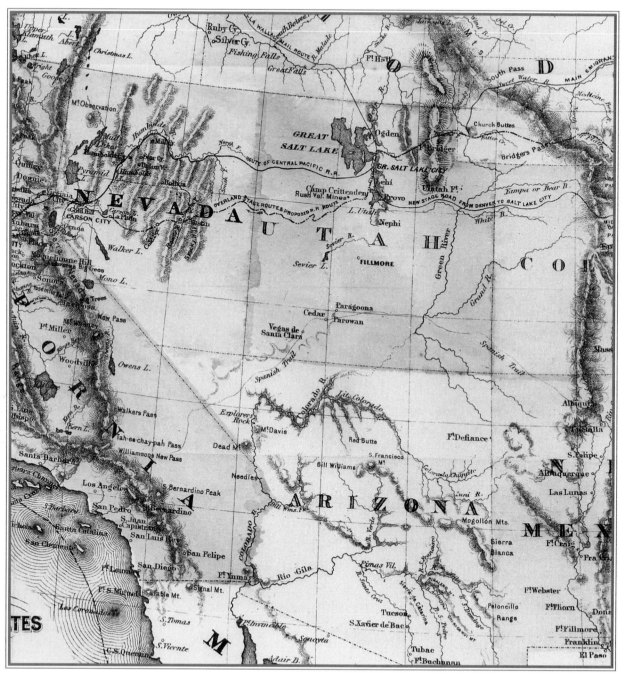

The western United States in a popular map printed in 1865. Big, or Grand, Canyon is situated where the label COLORADO R. *appears in northern Arizona. The dotted line is the presumed link between the Colorado River and the Green and Grand rivers to the northeast.*

down the Green River into the uncharted country that was thought to contain the steep canyons and fierce rapids of the Colorado. Ives had come up the river from its mouth and found it impassable. Why had no one attempted to explore it from the other direction, riding the current instead of fighting it? Perhaps someone had. In any event, the coming of the Transcontinental Railroad was a sure sign that the West could not keep this secret for long.

On May 10, Buffalo and the rest of the nation celebrated the driving of the golden spike that completed the Transcontinental Railroad. Three weeks later, Decoration Day came and with it several days of military parades and reunions. Then the circus arrived, baseball got started, strawberries ripened, and on June 29, high school graduation was held. The next day, with vacation under way at last, Fred was in the library reading a newspaper account of his school's commencement exercises when a small item caught his eye. There on the same page with the senior class roster was the following notice:

> *Advices from the Pacific slope report the loss of the*
> *Powell exploring party, with one exception, while*
> *attempting to cross the rapids of the Colorado River.*

That was all it said.

CHAPTER II
A Death-Defying Deed

July 1869

Hardly anybody could have been surprised by the unhappy fate of Powell's expedition. The West had swallowed up countless adventurers, just as Niagara Falls had claimed its share of daredevils. The surprise came a week later:

> The story of the loss of the Powell Expedition in the
> Colorado rapids is very generally discredited. A letter
> is published from Mrs. Powell, wife of Major Powell,
> the leader of the expedition, in which it is stated that
> no such man as Risdon, who reports himself the sole
> survivor, belonged to the party....

Here was a tale with a twist. Fred was consumed by several burning questions. Who was Major Powell? What was he trying to do? Where was he now? And who in the world was Risdon?

The question of Risdon was solved soon enough. As the story unfolded in the press, he turned out to be one of those all-too-common characters out west: a swindler. Hearing a rumor that Powell had met disaster while leading an expedition down the Green River to the Colorado, Risdon spread the story that he himself was the only survivor. He told a tale of Niagara-like rapids at a scary-sounding place called Brown's Hole, where a powerful whirlpool engulfed the explorers. The story was so thrilling that Risdon was given a free train ride back to his home in Illinois, which was probably his goal in concocting the hoax. Once there, he was caught stealing a horse and thrown in jail. Meanwhile, his tall tale was being disputed in the papers by Powell's wife, Emma, who was staying with relatives in Detroit. Also objecting was Professor Almon H. Thompson, Powell's brother-in-law and colleague at the Illinois Natural History Society, which was one of the sponsors of the expedition.

According to Emma, a letter had come from her husband dated *after* the supposed disaster. Furthermore the names of expedition members given by Risdon were, she said, "without a single exception," incorrect. Professor Thompson pointed out other discrepancies, such as confused geography and inaccurate personal details about Powell. "The whole tale is false and stamps John A. Risdon as an arrant liar or crazy person," he asserted.

Even as Emma and the professor were laying this yarn to rest, another "sole survivor" turned up. His story was just as full of holes as Risdon's and was likewise exposed. Nonetheless, Emma and the professor could not say whether Powell and his party were indeed safe, for the explorers were presumably deep in the mysterious canyon country of the Green River in eastern Utah, heading for the Colorado, where legend had it the river tumbled down mighty falls and disappeared into underground passages. If Brown's Hole had not swallowed them up, perhaps some other peril had.

The rumors, reports, and letters kept telegraph operators busy as they relayed news in Morse code from one newspaper to another around the country. About all that was known for certain was that Powell and nine men had started downriver in late May from Green River City, where the Transcontinental Railroad crossed the Green River just north of Utah Territory. The plan was to map the course of the river and explore its canyons. He would take up to ten months and end up below Big, or Grand, Canyon at the point where the Virgin River flowed in, which was about where Lieutenant Ives had abandoned his upstream investigation a decade earlier.

At least that was the plan as long as supplies held out. Considering the arid wilderness they were entering, the explorers would have few opportunities to replenish their provisions, and they would have even less chance to communicate with the outside world. But thanks to the publicity generated by the "sole survivors," any messages that did get out—through miners, mountain men, or Indians—would be eagerly read by an increasingly concerned nation. The concern would have been all the greater had it been widely known that the leader of this ultimate test of boating skill and endurance had only one arm.

Major John Wesley Powell was one of the many remarkable citizens that Illinois contributed to the Civil War. Like President Abraham Lincoln and General Ulysses S. Grant, who also hailed from the state, Powell was raised in hardship on the frontier, where an education was something a person had to create from scratch. In Powell's case, the raw materials were a love of the outdoors and a curiosity about everything in nature. His ambition to become a scientist was delayed by the war, which he entered in 1861 as a private. By the end of 1861, he was a captain. The following year, he was in the thick of action at the Battle of Shiloh when a bullet smashed his right arm. Afterward the arm was amputated above the elbow. Most soldiers would have quit at that point. Not Powell. He served at the Siege of Vicksburg and many other battles before finally resigning in 1865 with the permanent rank of major. It became his title—and his nickname—for life.

After the war, without even a college degree, Powell won a job as professor of natural science at an Illinois university. Fascinated with the geology of the West, he led several field trips to the Rocky Mountains. There he got the idea to try something no one had ever done: he would organize an expedition to explore the Colorado River canyons, the last unmapped region in the West. No one who knew his willingness to tackle a difficult job believed that the lack of an arm could affect his success in any way, not even on a wild, unknown river.

But where was he? On July 15, a report appeared about a group that had ventured down the Green River three weeks after the Major and had met fierce rapids. Their leader, a man named Hook, drowned. The survivors returned having seen no campsites, footprints, debris, or other signs of the Powell party. They seemed to have vanished without a trace.

Then two days later, a letter was printed in a Western newspaper from one of Powell's men. In the following days, letters from Powell himself and other expedition members were delivered to relatives, friends, and newspapers around the country. The mail had been sent in early July from the Ute Indian agency, a reservation trading post on one of the tributaries of the Green River, more than 200 river-miles from where the expedition had started. The explorers reported that all had gone well until June 7, when one of their four boats was crushed to pieces in a stretch of rapids that they immediately dubbed Disaster Falls. Although no one was hurt, they lost 2,000 pounds of supplies, including one third of their food. "The loss of the rations will compel us to shorten the time

Wreck at Disaster Falls in an engraving by American artist Thomas Moran, published in 1875.

for the work," Powell wrote, adding, "Personally I have enjoyed myself much, the scenery being wild and beautiful beyond description."

Another member of the party, who had been in the crushed boat, gave a more sober assessment: "Danger is our life."

August—September 1869

During August a few more letters were printed from the batch collected at the Ute agency. But the explorers had obviously long since left there. Both Emma and the professor assured friends that even with one third of the food gone, the party could still hold out until Christmas. Besides, before leaving the Major had said that five months instead of the allotted ten would probably be enough to run the canyons and obtain the data for a map, which was his main scientific goal. News of the expedition's success might therefore come as early as November.

At the end of August, Fred returned to school. Vacation had been the usual mix of excitement and boredom, inspiration and exhaustion. On August 7, there had been a partial eclipse of the sun in Buffalo, which everyone viewed through soot-blackened glass, ending up with smudged noses. There had also been the hoped-for stunt over Niagara Falls, though not quite what was advertised. An acrobat had claimed he would ride a velocipede across a rope strung over the chasm. As it happened, the vehicle was so securely bolted to the rope that it couldn't possibly fall off. Feeling cheated, spectators held higher hopes for another feat announced for later in the year, when a boat owner promised to send an old passenger barge, unoccupied, plunging down the rapids below the falls and into the notorious "Whirlpool." Fred wondered how that could possibly compare with real people running rapids on a river that had never been explored.

Then in mid-September there was an alarming newspaper report:

> *Three members of the Powell Expedition have been killed by the Indians.*

CHAPTER III
The Marvelous Major

September—October 1869

Fred was stunned. The first news of the Powell party since July, and it was only one sentence! But on the next page, in a column labeled BY TELEGRAPH THE MORNING'S DISPATCHES FROM NEW YORK, he found more information and an even bigger surprise:

> *According to a telegram the Powell Expedition*
> *arrived safely at the mouth of the Rio Virgin on the*
> *30th of August. Major Powell [is] on his way*
> *home....We have received a dispatch of the murder of*
> *three men belonging to the expedition....A friendly*
> *Indian has been sent out to get their papers....The*
> *telegraph does not give the names of the men.*

They had made it, months ahead of schedule! The three deaths were a shocking development, to be sure—all the more so since the details were so vague. Fred was reminded of battle reports during the Civil War, which rarely gave a clear picture of events until long after the action.

But he had to wait only two weeks for an official report from Major Powell himself, which the Buffalo paper headlined in grand style:

> *The Most Wonderful Scenery in the World—925*
> *Miles of Canyon and 300 Waterfalls—Rock Walls*
> *4,000 Feet High—Shooting Rapids and Cascades—*
> *Hair Breadth 'Scapes—Loss of Three Men—*
> *Ancient Indian Towns—A Fascinating Story.*

THE
WILD
COLORADO

Living up to the billing, Powell began:

In the great southwest region of the territory of the
United States there is a belt of country that has
long been the region of myths. Gorges with cliffs
overhanging to shut out the day; underground
courses of a great river that carries melted snows of
vast mountain cisterns; great cataracts, whose
plunging waters make roaring music, heard on the
distant mountain summits with a thousand
imaginative embellishments, have been given as the
characteristics of this region, known vaguely as the
Grand Canyon of the Colorado....

The Major went on to describe his research trips to the West to prepare for the voyage, the special design of his four boats, his crew of nine mountain men and adventurers, and the expedition itself—through canyons far more marvelous and dangerous than myth or the ominously blank regions of maps could suggest. Where rumor had placed an unbroken canyon system extending for nearly a thousand miles down the Green and Colorado rivers, Powell found a series of distinctly different canyons, whose characteristics depended on the type of rock in each. He gave them stark, descriptive names: Desolation, Coal, Stillwater, Cataract, Narrow, Mound, Monument, Marble—and, most wonderful of all, Grand, as he settled on calling the legendary chasm that Ives and a handful of others had glimpsed. No American explorer had ever seen the Grand Canyon from one end to the other, as Powell and his crew had—or at least, as *some* of his crew had.

Powell reported that one of his men had deserted early in the expedition. And he told how three others mutinied at the grimmest stretch of rapids, deep in the Grand Canyon. Up to that point things had gone reasonably well. Except for the smashed boat, the explorers had successfully run hundreds of rapids, always approaching them with great caution

Major John Wesley Powell.

and, where possible, walking the boats around the most dangerous sections. There had been no shortage of hair-raising rides—but nothing like what they encountered now, as they faced a nearly unbroken stretch of furious white water, three quarters of a mile long, hemmed in by cliffs, with no way to carry the boats around the deadly obstacle course.

They were dangerously short of food, for in addition to the lost provisions aboard the wrecked boat, they were losing supplies to spoilage from constant drenching. Having long since abandoned his plan to conduct a careful scientific survey, Powell was dedicated simply to getting through the canyons alive.

After landing the boats to survey the rapids ahead, he decided that the best option was to ride through, come what may. Three of his men disagreed. That evening they announced they would climb out and risk their luck finding a settlement beyond the mountains. Powell tried to talk them out of it, arguing that the rough patch ahead was surely one of the last before they emerged from the canyon and completed the voyage. But the men could not be convinced. The next morning they packed a few belongings, said good-bye, and began winding their way up the cliffs on the north side of the canyon.

Powell and the five who remained chose two boats, leaving one behind in case the others returned. Then they headed into the rapids on what seemed like a suicide mission. But their boating skill got them through, stunned and soaked, but alive. They landed at the first opportunity, bailed out, and fired shots into the air, hoping their departing comrades would hear and rejoin them. "But we never saw nor heard of them since," Powell reported.

He didn't say it, but he left the reader to conclude that these were the three who were found dead in the desert.

Fall 1869—Winter 1870

The Major returned east to a hero's welcome. On November 9, he gave a public lecture in his wife's hometown of Detroit. Searching for a way to give his audience a true impression of the scale of the Grand Canyon, he asked them to imagine a gorge a mile deep, in places no wider than a street, extending from Detroit to Chicago. They were electrified. He described the human drama of the trip, which was as thrilling as any novel. But he also recounted the scientific story of how this remarkable natural wonder came to be.

It had all been done by water, he said. Snow fell in the mountains that ringed the canyon country. In springtime the snow melted, creating torrential streams that fed the rivers and eroded the land. "The beautiful clouds!" he exclaimed. "They have carved out the mountains! They give us the beauty of the heavens. They give us all that is sublime...for without them there would be no mountains that are grand, no landscape that is beautiful!" Powell's presentation was an adventure story, a science lesson, and a poetry talk all wrapped into one. During the fall and winter he lectured throughout the Midwest, where he was compared with the great Scottish explorer of Africa, Dr. David Livingstone:

Prof. J. W. Powell
will deliver his Lecture on
The Canyons of the Colorado

This lecture reveals a new and unique country. It describes the greatest physical wonder on the Continent. It narrates the most thrilling journey of the century. What Livingstone's exploration of the sources of the Nile is to Africa, Major Powell's discovery is to North America.

Price of admission, 50 cents

Even at fifty cents per person, the price of a meal at an expensive restaurant, halls were packed. But the Major was not getting rich with these events; he was raising funds for his next trip. He reported that much had been left undone during his hurried voyage, and he intended to go back. After each lecture young men invariably stepped forward to volunteer their services—offers that the Major always politely declined.

Unfortunately, Buffalo was not on Powell's lecture circuit, and Fred saw news reports gradually disappear. But as good luck would have it, he discovered an entirely new source of information, for it turned out that an old family friend, Dr. John Bell, had served with Major Powell in the Union army.

CHAPTER IV
A Fateful Meeting

April 5, 1871

"Do you travel far, lad?" The sun glinted from the ice on Lake Erie, flooding the cars of the Pacific Express with light as the train made its way westward from Buffalo, New York, toward the land of real buffalo.

"Yes, sir," answered Fred. "I'm going to Chicago." He was seated next to a married couple, who seemed even more alert to the sights and sounds around them than Fred was himself.

The husband continued, "They say Chicago is a remarkable city."

"Yes, sir. It's an exciting place," agreed Fred, warming to a subject he loved. "Everybody is busy day and night. I expect it will have grown a lot since I was there last summer." He was going to Chicago for the second time since his *Fountain City* excursion nearly three years before. It had been almost two years since he spent a lazy summer in Buffalo following the exploits of Major Powell. Much had happened since then. He was now a senior in high school, though at the moment he was absent from classes—with his parents' permission.

"Are you traveling to Chicago yourselves?" Fred asked politely.

"My wife and I are staying only a few days," said the man, "then we resume our journey to the Pacific."

"I hope to travel to the West myself," said Fred. He paused, then added, "It all depends on how my interview goes."

The man's wife looked at the boy. As if guessing his mission, she blurted, "Oh, you're joining the pony express!"

"But, my dear," interrupted her husband, "you know that the overland mail riders were put out of business long ago."

"I was just thinking he *looks* like a pony express rider," explained the wife, who held a thick guidebook. She proceeded to tell the history of

*Fred Dellenbaugh
in 1870.*

the pony express and its mostly teenage riders, rumored to have been recruited from the ranks of orphans because of the great dangers of the job.

In fact, Fred had once dreamed of doing this very thing. But now he was pursuing a different quest. "Ma'am," he said when she was finished, "I hope to do something a thousand times more exciting." And he described how he was on his way to Chicago to meet Major John Wesley Powell, having heard that the famous explorer needed crew members for his repeat voyage through the Colorado canyons, due to depart in less than a month.

"Oh, my!" exclaimed the woman.

"That would be quite an adventure," agreed her husband, who immediately turned practical. "I don't want to dash your hopes, son. But I would expect that Major Powell could fill his party with men of much wider experience than you are likely to have—judging by your age."

"True," admitted Fred. "But he has already selected his scientists, his surveyors, his photographer. These are all men who served in the war, and they are his officers. But he also needs soldiers—men to pull the oars and assist with every other job. Not just strong fellows, but smart fellows."

"Well, you are obviously both," said the man generously. "Good luck to you!"

Fred hoped that Major Powell saw it that way, too. Dr. Bell had telegraphed his old army friend to arrange the meeting, recommending Fred as a good boatman and a quick learner. He didn't mention that Fred was only seventeen.

Fred had heard about the opening from Frank Richardson, a boy not much older than himself, whom he had met in Chicago the previous summer. At that time, Fred had not thought about Major Powell or the Colorado for quite a while. But the subject unexpectedly came up as he was getting to know Richardson, who, it turned out, knew the Powell family. Richardson filled in his new acquaintance on the Major's whereabouts. He explained that the explorer was back in the West laying the groundwork for a second voyage down the Colorado and trying to learn the circumstances concerning the murder of his three men.

A few months later, Fred got a remarkable letter from Richardson. The Chicago youth revealed that Major Powell had selected him as a boatman and general assistant for the upcoming second expedition. He

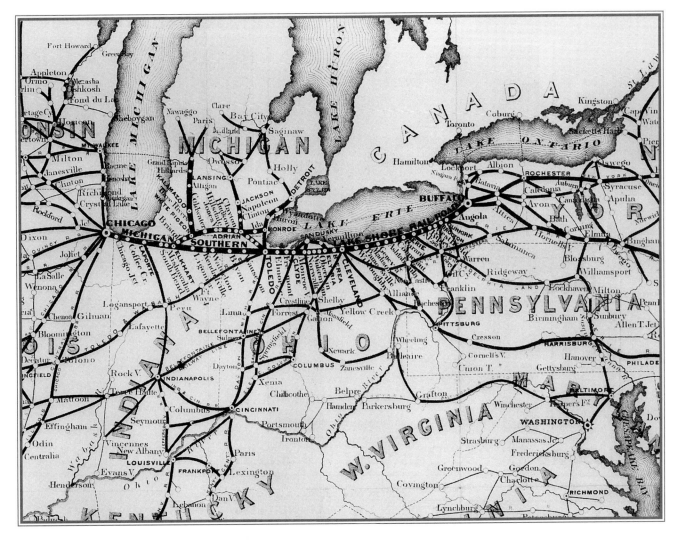

even hinted that one or two places might still be open! Acting quickly, Fred contacted Dr. Bell, who immediately telegraphed a letter of recommendation. The Major wired back, agreeing to meet the promising young man from Buffalo.

Back aboard the train, the woman was assuring Fred that of course he would be selected, and she began filling him in on what to expect. Her guidebook was short on information about the Colorado, but it was full of material on Indians, outlaws, wild animals, miners, and Mormons. She

Heading west. Fred's train route from Buffalo, New York, to Chicago, Illinois, via the Lake Shore and Michigan Southern Railway, 1871.

was particularly interested in the Mormons, a religious sect that had settled the area around the Great Salt Lake in Utah. By all accounts these pious people had created prosperity in the midst of desolation. And yet they had strange and sometimes ruthless ways. She and her husband would be visiting Salt Lake City, and she was especially concerned about an awful massacre said to have been organized by Mormon leaders against a band of California-bound immigrants many years before. The United States government was still trying to make a case against those responsible....

But Fred had stopped listening, for he was rehearsing the case he himself would soon be making.

April 7, 1871

"Tell me, how is Bell?" inquired Major Powell as he reached out and clasped the back of Fred's outstretched hand. It hadn't occurred to the boy that greeting someone having no right arm required a change in the usual procedure. The famous explorer was about Fred's height, though more solidly built. He sported a full ruddy beard, and his suit was rough, befitting a man more at home in the splendorous works of nature than in the fancy Chicago hotel where they were meeting.

They talked of their mutual friend Dr. Bell for several minutes, giving Fred the distinct feeling that the Major was reluctant to move on to the purpose of the interview.

"So, you want to join the expedition," he said at last. "To be honest, ours is a very small party, ten including myself. There is scarcely room for more in our three boats, once all the equipment is loaded." He paused and scratched his beard. "It's true that I shall probably need one more crewman. But I had thought of enlisting someone who wouldn't need much breaking in."

"Major Powell, I've been broken in by the Niagara River, which has the roughest current this side of the Rockies," insisted Fred, a bit desperately.

"Have you run the falls, then?"

Fred wasn't sure if the Major was joking. "No, sir. No one has done that and lived to tell about it. I've handled small boats in the swift water above the falls…and in the choppy water of Lake Erie."

"It seems to me that the Colorado is more like the water *below* Niagara Falls," observed the Major, "with rapids, whirlpools, and boulders ready to dash a fellow to pieces. String a thousand such places together and that's what the Colorado is."

"I don't doubt it, sir, but I think I'm strong enough and quick enough to handle it."

"Suppose you are—what else are you good at?"

Fred had never been on a camping trip, so he didn't want to bring that up. "I'm a good shot, I can patch a boat and carve an oar, I can swim….I've been through most of high school….I can draw…."

"You can draw?" Powell seemed interested.

"Yes, sir. It's my hobby. I like to draw things in nature."

"Well, that we shall need. Tell me more about your hobbies."

Fred swallowed hard and described his literary activities. During the past year, he and a friend had published a monthly boys' magazine devoted to adventure stories and short articles on events around Buffalo. Much of each issue was written by Fred himself.

"I am fond of literature myself," said the Major, more enthusiastically than Fred expected. "I have used it many, many times to ward off loneliness in the wild."

Fred wondered what kind of literature he meant.

"How old are you, Fred?"

"Eighteen come September, sir."

"Well, that makes you seventeen, doesn't it?" He scratched his beard. "Just my age when I set off on my first big adventure—not as big an adventure as this, mind you." He smiled. "Well, Fred, I guess you will do."

One of Fred's first sketches
for Major Powell, showing
Monument Butte at Green
River City, April 29, 1871.
The same feature is in the
background of the photo on
page 8.

CHAPTER V
Getting Ready

April 29, 1871

Fred sat on a rock amid the sagebrush and greasewood in Green River City, sketching a towering butte just north of the town. "Former town" would more accurately describe the nearly abandoned settlement. Just a few years earlier it had been a thriving community during construction of the Transcontinental Railroad. Now it was little more than a station stop and a store, surrounded by mostly empty shanties.

Two of the shanties were being occupied by the personnel of Powell's Second Colorado River Exploring Expedition, newly arrived that very morning. Besides Fred, Major Powell, and Richardson, there were seven other men and two women, plus three boats and several tons of supplies. Following a sumptuous breakfast at Field's Outfitting Store—at fifty cents per person—the party began preparations for the forthcoming voyage, still many days away.

Assigned as expedition artist, Fred was busy practicing the skill that would have to become second nature to him: making a quick visual record of anything the Major and his fellow scientists needed for reference.

Major Powell's second-in-command was his brother-in-law, Professor Thompson. This was the same scientist who had served as a spokesman back in Illinois during the first expedition. Called "Prof" by the men, he would be responsible for producing the first detailed maps of the Green and Colorado canyons. He would be aided by Captain Francis Bishop, called "Cap," who was a college science teacher, and by Steven Jones, a school principal who was an experienced surveyor.

Emma Dean Powell, the Major's wife, was present. So was Nellie Powell Thompson, who was Prof's wife and the Major's sister. The two women were helping with preparations and would soon travel to Salt

Lake City to establish an administrative base and deliver Emma's impending baby. It would be the first child for the Major and Emma, who had been married nine years and had shared many adventures. Emma was at the Major's side when his bullet-shattered arm had to be amputated after Shiloh. She had also accompanied him on his trips out west to prepare for the first river voyage. During one of these, she had become the first woman to climb Pike's Peak. As for Nellie, she loved the outdoors as much as her brother, the Major, and like him was fascinated with science—her specialty being plants. The two women would stay in Salt Lake City until after the baby's birth and then rejoin the expedition—with the baby—at winter headquarters in southern Utah.

In addition to his duty as commander, the Major was also chief geologist. In this capacity he was assisted by John Steward, an old army acquaintance. Eight years earlier, the two had met while hunting fossils in the trenches outside of Vicksburg during the long wait for the beleaguered city to surrender. In fact, Steward was already finding fossils in the sandstone bluffs near Green River City. Steward's assistant was Richardson, who unfortunately was distracted by having accidentally sliced off the end of his thumb while on the train the previous day.

Fred's drawings would be supplemented by even better pictures made by E. O. Beaman, an experienced photographer from New York City. Beaman was just now unpacking more than a thousand pounds of equipment, including an unwieldy camera, a portable darkroom called a "blind box," bottles of chemicals, developing trays, and hundreds of glass plates for negatives. His assistant was Clem Powell, the Major's twenty-one-year-old cousin, who was as keen about literature and the outdoors as Fred. Clem was at pains not to exploit his relationship with the Major, since he wanted to be treated no differently from the other men. With Nellie, though, he was full of fun and jokes; the two were obviously devoted cousins.

Andy Hattan was assigned as cook, even though he had no experience in the subject. But the Major had every confidence in his abilities, having served with him in the war. Indeed, with the exception of Fred,

Richardson, and Clem, who had been too young to participate, all the men had served in the war.

They would all serve at the oars, too, for the Major was counting on each man to either row or work a steering oar. Jack Sumner was assigned as first mate in charge of the boat crews. An expert wilderness guide, he had been on the first expedition and was the only veteran besides the Major to be repeating the trip. But he had not yet arrived in Green River City from his winter camp in the Rocky Mountains.

Green River City, May 4, 1871. Field's Outfitting Store is the building at the right, with a plank reading RESTAURANT above the door.

May 8, 1871

A week later, the members of the party learned that Sumner would not be coming. A late-season snowstorm had trapped him in the high country. Therefore the Major and Prof decided to recruit a replacement in Salt Lake City, where they had gone to conduct some last-minute business.

Unable to draw on Sumner's experiences firsthand, the men back in Green River City could at least consult his diary from the first voyage, which featured such passages as these:

> *Had another narrow escape today....Came very near being drawn into a rapid that would smash any boat to pieces....Drifted three quarters of a mile through a perfect hell of waves. Came to a rapid that cannot be run by any boat....Ran three very dangerous rapids...boat was swamped again....Ran six bad rapids....Ran 13 rapids....Ran 31 rapids....*

"'Tis enough to make one's hair stand on end,'" Clem confided in his own diary. If the others had reservations, they didn't show it, except for Richardson, who was obviously scared out of his wits and talked openly of backing out.

May 16, 1871

On this day the Major made crew assignments, signaling that departure was near. The previous day he and Prof had returned from Salt Lake City with Sumner's substitute, a German-born immigrant and former soldier in the West named Jack Hillers. Though not a mountain man, Hillers was smart, capable, cheerful, and likely to make a dependable general assistant. The Major must have thought very highly of him, for Hillers was assigned to row the aft oars in the Major's own boat, the *Emma Dean* (named for Mrs. Powell).

The other boats were the *Nellie Powell* (named for Mrs. Thompson) and the *Cañonita* (Spanish for "little canyon"). All three were of identical design and had been custom-built in Chicago to the Major's specifications. Constructed of half-inch-thick oak planks and double-ribbed for strength, they were probably the finest river-running craft ever made. Each was twenty-two feet long and five and one-quarter feet across at the widest point. The hull was completely decked over except for cockpits fore and aft for the oarsmen. These were sealed off by bulkheads, providing three watertight cabins for cargo and for buoyancy. Not even a capsizing could sink the vessel or harm its contents—unless of course holes were stove in by sharp blows from rocks, which was certainly a possibility. The design was similar to that used on the first expedition, except that Powell had made improvements in the strength and storage capacity of the vessels. Since the boats were better, he trusted the same held for the crews.

Completing the personnel of the *Emma Dean* were Jones, who would handle the eighteen-foot-long steering oar, and Fred himself, who would work the forward oars. Fred felt doubly honored. By occupying the forward spot in the lead boat, he would be literally the first to encounter any dangers. He would also have an unrivaled opportunity to talk to the Major, who would be only a few feet away, facing him from the deck of the middle cabin.

Nellie Powell was to be steered by Prof, with Steward rowing aft and Cap forward. Richardson was stationed on the deck of the middle cabin with no particular duties, the only crewman so assigned.

Cañonita would have Beaman at the helm. He had once been a ship pilot on the Great Lakes. Andy would row aft and Clem forward. There was no fourth man on this boat.

May 22, 1871

The provisions were packed; the scientific instruments were tested and stowed; rifles for each man were loaded and at the ready; a shipment of extra-heavy oars had arrived from Chicago and were installed in the oarlocks, replacing sweeps broken during practice runs; an old wooden armchair from Field's Store was lashed to the deck of the *Emma Dean* as a

A formal portrait on the day of crew assignments, May 16, 1871. Left to right: Andy Hattan, Clem Powell, and E. O. Beaman in the Cañonita. *Stephen Jones, Jack Hillers, Major Powell, and Fred Dellenbaugh in the* Emma Dean. *Prof Thompson, John Steward, Cap Bishop, and Frank Richardson in the* Nellie Powell. *At the left is Beaman's "blind box" for coating and developing photographic plates.*

First camp, Green River City, May 1871. Left to right: Prof, Andy, Jones, Steward, Clem, Richardson, Fred, and Cap.

crow's-nest for the Major; and at seven A.M., the explorers were assembled at Field's, consuming a hearty farewell breakfast.

Powell had briefed the men on his plans—although these were just as likely to change as his schedule on the first trip. As everyone knew, that voyage had been thrown off track by the smash-up of a boat, the loss of most of the food, and the desertion of the three men who were later found dead. Barring a repeat of such disasters, Powell intended to spend roughly six months on the Green and Colorado rivers, exploring and mapping to just above the Grand Canyon. He had arranged for supplies to be delivered to the expedition by Mormon packers at several points along the way. Facing the onset of winter, the explorers would then cache their boats and head overland to the Mormon settlement of Kanab in southern Utah. There, they would be joined by Nellie, Emma, and the new baby. Using Kanab as a base, the explorers would investigate the surrounding countryside, large parts of which were unrecorded on any map. Come spring, they would retrieve the boats and float through the Grand Canyon to the Virgin River and perhaps to the mouth of the Colorado itself, where it emptied into the Gulf of California.

The Major was already three weeks behind his schedule when the party finally departed at ten A.M., under a brilliant blue sky, with Green River City's entire citizenry—about fifteen people—all cheering. All, that is, except for two boys who put on a gruesome pantomime of the fate they predicted for the explorers: capsized boats, flailing arms, and death by drowning.

It was the last thing Fred saw as the *Emma Dean* rounded the first bend...toward who could imagine what adventures?

CHAPTER VI
Downriver

Later that night

Fred had never expected this! Indians were trying to steal the boats! He groped in the darkness for his rifle but couldn't find it. Shouting to warn his sleeping comrades, he sprang for the nearest intruder and pinned him to the ground by the throat. The culprit struggled, crying out in a strangely familiar voice.

It was Jones! As the gasping man's face and form came into focus— along with the startled sleepers scrambling from their bedrolls around the smoldering campfire—Fred suddenly realized that he had been having a nightmare. He let go of Jones and tried to explain. The men laughed, made a few jokes, and were soon snoring again.

Gazing up at the thickening clouds on this, his first night ever in the open, Fred thought about the day's almost effortless progress down the river. The most memorable moment had not been a fierce rapid but a sandbar that had briefly stranded the boats. Now this had happened! He scolded himself for being so jumpy. Still awake, he began to wonder what *had* happened to his rifle. Searching around, he finally found it. He pulled it up close and fell deeply back asleep.

May 23–June 1, 1871

They were awakened before dawn by a cold rain. It soon turned to snow, falling thick and fast. The men retreated to a tiny, abandoned cabin nearby. Andy made a roaring fire and prepared a breakfast of bread, bacon, and coffee. When all was ready, he lifted the food from the coals with his old hat and announced, "Well, go for it, boys!"—which they did. A few hours later, with the snow still falling, he made an identical meal for lunch—equally appreciated.

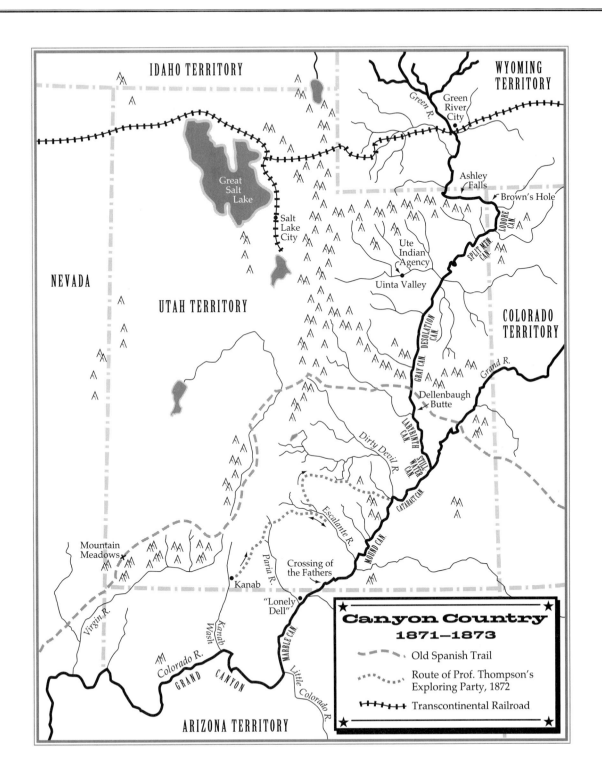

IDAHO TERRITORY

WYOMING TERRITORY

Green R.

Green River City

Ashley Falls

Brown's Hole

Great Salt Lake

Salt Lake City

LODORE CAN.

SPLIT MTN. CAN.

Ute Indian Agency

Uinta Valley

NEVADA

UTAH TERRITORY

COLORADO TERRITORY

DESOLATION CAN.

GRAY CAN.

Grand R.

Dellenbaugh Butte

LABYRINTH CAN.

STILL WATER CAN.

Dirty Devil R.

CATARACT CAN.

Escalante R.

MOUND CAN.

Mountain Meadows

Paria R.

Crossing of the Fathers

Kanab

"Lonely Dell"

Virgin R.

Kanab Wash

Colorado R.

GRAND   CANYON

MARBLE CAN.

Little Colorado R.

ARIZONA TERRITORY

Canyon Country
1871–1873

— — — Old Spanish Trail

· · · · · Route of Prof. Thompson's Exploring Party, 1872

+++++ Transcontinental Railroad

The weather cleared in the afternoon and the explorers continued downriver. They encountered a party of fur trappers. Steward had already collected a box of fossils, and the trappers agreed to take them back to Green River City for shipment east. The others were also busy with their duties, taking advantage of the smooth water to master their routines. Fred's assignment was to make a continuous drawing of the river's left wall, all the way to the Grand Canyon. For this purpose, he kept a sketchbook in a waterproof pocket on the bulkhead in front of him to use when he wasn't rowing.

Prof, Cap, and Jones were to record the course and width of the stream, estimating the distances between compass bearings, and gauging the height of the canyon walls. As they continued downriver, whenever the boats stopped, one of the three men would usually climb the cliffs to make a rough map of the surrounding countryside.

Beaman, too, went on these hikes, with as many assistants as he could enlist—to lug the camera strongbox, the chemical and plateholder box, and the blind box. Once he decided on a view, he had to set up the tripod, aim and focus the camera, set up the blind box, coat a glass plate with toxic chemicals to make it light-sensitive, load the plate into its holder, insert the holder into the camera, uncap the lens for several seconds to several minutes depending on the brightness of the scene, then develop and process the negative. If the picture didn't come out, he had to repeat the entire procedure. Finally, he had to take down the equipment and move on to the next viewpoint.

The Major hadn't faced the boatload of photo supplies and bothersome procedures on his first trip, since he didn't have a photographer. But he was sure it was worth it now. Only photography could convince people that the spectacular painted views of the West that they had seen in art galleries and illustrated books were, in fact, near the truth. Not only would photographs lend a sense of reality to the Major's amazing exploits, but he planned to sell copies of the pictures to raise funds for more exploits.

While most of the men were settling into their duties, Richardson was having trouble with his. Geology didn't interest him, and he resented the exhausting outings with Steward and the Major, collecting rocks that scarcely seemed to differ from one another. One day he wandered away from a field trip. Powell was furious and threatened to give him five days' rations and send him back to Green River City for desertion. The boy was happiest hunting or playing the flute that he had brought along. He enjoyed outdoor life, but the rigors of a scientific expedition and the stress of waiting for catastrophe on the deck of a boat where he had nothing to do were beginning to wear him down.

He was also tiring of the food, for every meal was the same: bread, coffee, bacon or beans, and fresh meat only when there was time to stop and hunt, which wasn't often enough to suit Richardson.

June 2, 1871

"Here she comes!" shouted the Major. It was the first bad rapid, proclaimed by an awesome roar emerging from a point ahead where the Green River suddenly narrowed. *Emma Dean* was the first through, rocking and tossing on the mad waters. Veering to avoid a sunken boulder, she sideswiped a cliff and smashed Hillers' starboard oarlock. With only one working oar, Hillers couldn't row, and the task of propelling the boat to safety fell to Fred. Meanwhile, the Major was signaling vigorously for the other boats to avoid the spot. But the crew of the *Nellie Powell* misunderstood, and Fred saw her crash and capsize.

Pulling mightily, Fred drove the *Emma Dean* toward a little beach. As she scraped bottom, the men leaped out and pulled her ashore. Seconds later, the *Cañonita* joined them, landing just downstream, unscathed under Beaman's expert piloting. But the *Nellie Powell*—with Prof, Steward, Cap, and Richardson—was nowhere to be seen.

Andy tried to wade upstream to investigate, but he was stopped by the torrent. Clambering over the cliffs, the Major got a glimpse of some survivors. He shouted to them and got a reply. About an hour later, the *Nellie Powell* came racing down, apparently none the worse for wear.

Prof explained that she had struck a boulder broadside, flipped over, and spilled Richardson. The rest managed to scramble onto rocks. Acting quickly, Prof grabbed Richardson before he was swept away. Steward grabbed the boat, and Cap grabbed the towline, securing it to a tree. Then they hauled *Nellie Powell* ashore and made repairs on the spot. All they lost were a kettle, a sponge, a compass, and their dignity—for they now had the distinction of being the first crew to be dunked.

Emma Dean's damage was also quickly repaired, and the entire party set forth again. Alert to the prospect of more adventure, Fred focused his attention on the next awesome roar ahead, surprised at his eagerness to face more danger.

June 4, 1871

Some spots were too rough even for Powell, and the men frequently resorted to portages. In a regular portage, the cargo was unloaded, and the boats and goods were laboriously carried along the shore. Whenever possible, the Major preferred a line portage, also called a letdown, in which fully loaded boats were guided through the water one at a time, with two men on board to protect and steer the craft, and three or four others straining from the bank on hundred-foot-long ropes attached fore and aft to keep the craft from breaking free. A line portage was faster than the regular kind, but far more dangerous and exhausting.

After a letdown around one rough patch, the men reboarded and ran a small rapid. They shortly came to a place where the river narrowed and sent up another deafening roar. Looking it over, the Major judged it passable, and they quickly shot through in a fury of spray. They were getting the hang of it. Such rides usually left the cockpits full of water. But the sealed cargo cabins kept the boats afloat, and the men simply bailed out with kettles and hats when they had a chance.

Eventually they came to the wrecks of three boats half-buried in the sand. Searching the area, Jones discovered a grave with a pine board bearing the name of Hook. This was the man who had led a party down the Green River shortly after Powell's first expedition had set forth.

Jones, Hillers, and Fred engaged in a "letdown" around a patch of bad rapids, June 1871.

Ashley Falls in Beaman's photo and Fred's drawing, June 5, 1871. The photo is made from the left bank of the river, downstream of the falls. Note the boat at the lower right. Fred's sketch is made from the other bank, looking across the falls toward the rock slide where ASHLEY 1825 *was painted halfway up the hillside.*

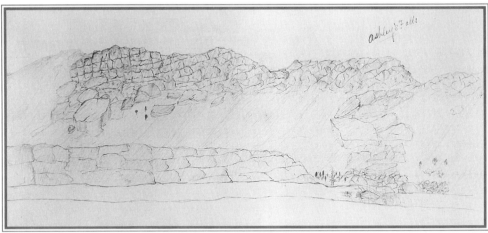

Clearly the group had given up here after losing their leader. "It's a shame about Hook," said the Major sadly. "But it saved the others. The rapids downriver would have killed them all."

The men nodded respectfully. Richardson began to shake.

June 5–7, 1871

They came to a spot where an enormous landslide had tumbled into the river, creating a natural dam. The fall over the dam, about eight feet, was too dangerous to risk even a letdown—as the men discovered when they tried it and almost destroyed a boat. So they carried the other two boats along the bank. On one of these trips, Fred made a detour to look for an inscription that Powell had found on the earlier voyage. Halfway up the hillside was a boulder with large black letters: ASHLEY 1825. The Major suspected that Ashley was a hunter who had once traveled this far down-river and called it quits—not that he couldn't have gone farther, since, according to the Major, there was nothing but smooth water for many miles ahead.

Over the next two days, Powell's assurance seemed like a grim joke as the men faced one fierce rapid after another. "Any more smooth water up ahead, Major?" shouted Hillers over the spray.

"About the same, Jack," said Powell from his chair.

June 8, 1871

Here at last was the Major's smooth water, leading into a protected mountain valley that hunters called a hole. It was Brown's Hole, named for an early trapper, and it was the spot where Risdon had set his tall tale about the loss of the first expedition. For Risdon, *hole* suggested a per-ilous place. In fact, it was exactly the opposite. The term signified a snug spot protected from harsh mountain weather. Providing grass for animals and refuge from the elements, such features were the preferred meeting grounds for trappers, Indians, prospectors, herders, and anyone else in the high country. Nonetheless, the Major felt that *hole* suggested some-thing unpleasant, so he renamed it Brown's Park.

Here the explorers encountered a group of cowboys camped by the river with 2,000 head of Texas cattle destined for the Pacific coast. Several of the cowboys had recently come overland from Green River City, where they had been given mail to deliver to the Major—if they ever saw him.

Cowboys at Brown's Park, June 1871.

Since some of the men would soon be heading back to Green River City, they offered to take any letters from the Major and his men.

Seizing the opportunity, Powell declared a bivouac to relax, write home, and bring the expedition's records up to date. He also decided that Richardson had to go. He realized that he had made a mistake in choosing this particular young man, who probably wouldn't survive the dangers ahead.

Fred was shocked at his friend's dismissal, though most of the others were not surprised. Trying to make the best of it, Cap arranged to barter Steward's pistol for Richardson's flute. The men had firearms aplenty but would sorely miss the only musical instrument in camp besides a harmonica brought by Fred and played almost exclusively by Steward. But first Cap, old soldier that he was, couldn't resist firing a few rounds to demonstrate the pistol. Unfortunately the barrel burst, and the trade was off.

A few days later, Richardson was off, too, and the party was down to ten.

CHAPTER VII
Poems and Perils

June 13, 1871

Viewing the mountain's ridge askance,
The Saxon stood in sullen trance,
Till Moray pointed with his lance,
    And cried—"Behold yon isle!"

Reading the stirring passage aloud, the Major made a dramatic flourish, which was tricky since he held the poetry book in his only hand. Not that there were any islands to point to at that particular moment, though there were ridges aplenty—no end of them, looming all around as the *Emma Dean*, *Nellie Powell*, and *Cañonita* drifted quietly through Brown's Park toward the magnificent Gates of Lodore.

Steward and Andy were swimming alongside, and the others were resting on the boats, which had been tied together to make a raft. At the center sat the Major in his chair, performing *The Lady of the Lake*, Sir Walter Scott's epic poem of Scottish knights and wars. The men watched and listened, mesmerized by the gripping tale.

On the earlier voyage one of the crewmen had named the stunning chasm ahead after *The Cataract of Lodore* by the English poet Robert Southey. A cataract was a great rush of water, which was certainly a familiar phenomenon to the men. So was poetry. It seemed as if everyone in the United States loved poetry—the way it captured experiences in memorable language. Southey managed to make his poem sound like flowing water itself:

The cataract strong
Then plunges along,
Striking and raging
As if a war raging
Its caverns and rocks among;
Rising and leaping,
Sinking and creeping,
Swelling and sweeping,
Showering and springing,
Flying and flinging…

…and so on with more than a hundred ringing, winging, playing, spraying, sounding, bounding, gripping, tripping, disarming, and alarming descriptions of the inimitable "way the water comes down at Lodore." Southey meant the Lodore of his imagination, but it fit the one ahead perfectly.

The Major also had a volume of Shakespeare, which became a favorite of Clem's, who was working his way through all the plays and had found this stirring passage in *King Lear:*

Blow, winds, and crack your cheeks. Rage, blow.
You cataracts and hurricanoes, spout
Till you have drenched our steeples, drowned the cocks….

Strange how a poet could capture the drama of a moment. At quiet times on the river or by the campfire, the men found that poetry was the perfect way to appreciate sights and sounds that seemed almost beyond belief.

June 16, 1871

After several days of rest and easy boating in Brown's Park, with plenty of time for side trips, the explorers arrived at the Gates of Lodore. The cowboys were still just a few miles off and promised to make one last mail call to pick up letters. In the dying firelight on the night before the next dangerous phase of the trip, Fred penned a message to his younger sister back in Buffalo:

> *Dear Belle,*
>
> *Here we are at the mouth of "Lodore," one of the grandest and most magnificent canyons on the river and containing some of the finest scenery in the world. Its red sandstone walls rise abruptly like a huge gateway to the height of about twenty-five hundred feet. From our camp we can see about a quarter of a mile into its almost indescribably grand depths….I have been working at my sketch of the valley of Brown's Park and mending my shoes, all day, so have to-night to write in and our camp-fire isn't very bright so you must not wonder at the crookedness of the lines, for lying on the ground beside a dim camp-fire is not very convenient. I have written a couple of letters to Dr. Bell since we started, to let him know how things are prospering….I had a long tramp and climb with Steward day before yesterday. We started out about eight o'clock prepared for a two-day's camp and climb. We crossed the valley to the mountains and had but one canteen of water….*

Fred continued with a suspenseful tale in which he and Steward made the classic wilderness mistake of failing to mark the spot where they left their packs and rifles. After going hungry for twenty-four hours, they finally located the provisions. Fred closed with a postscript:

> *P.S. …That rifle is quite a comfort out here. I can go to sleep with that by my side and feel that at any*

Fred's sketch mentioned in the letter to his sister dated June 16, 1871. The view is from a mountain overlooking Brown's Park, where Fred had gone the previous day. The Gates of Lodore are at the extreme right.

moment I can put in my seventeen shots in double-quick time....The [photographs] that Mr. Beaman makes will form one of the finest collections in the world and will be worth looking at. About five hundred of the best will form quite a study which with my sketches and the Major's report will give one a pretty good idea of this Western Country, though you can imagine huge mountains and a river set down in the midst of a vast wilderness of dry stunted sagebrush and sand....My love to all.

Fred

June 17–25, 1871

Lodore was nine days of nearly nonstop rapids—the worst twenty-mile stretch on the Green River, according to the Major. The ordeal included such perilous passages as Disaster Falls, where a boat had been crushed during the first expedition, a wild descent called Triplet Falls, and an immensely long chute of seething foam that Steward named Hell's Half-Mile.

It all started quietly enough, with the current drifting gently through a spectacular pair of gates. These consisted of two sides of a mountain split in half by the river. It was proof, said Powell, that the river was there before the mountain. As the land rose with imperceptible slowness, the stream stayed where it was, carving a channel that grew deeper and deeper, like a buzz saw cutting through a log.

Powell gave Fred many such geology lessons as they went. While Fred sketched, Powell would identify rock types in the cliffs and have Fred make notations on his drawings. Strung end to end, the drawings would permit scientists back east to take a complete voyage down the river without ever leaving their chairs.

During these chats Powell reminisced about his own experiences, which is how Fred learned the circumstances of the deaths of the three members of the first expedition. A year after that voyage, Powell had traveled to the region north of the Grand Canyon with Jacob Hamblin—a famous Mormon scout—to learn what local Indians knew about the massacre. As it happened, he and Hamblin ended up staying with the very tribe that had committed the act. They were Shiwits, and although Powell could not speak their language, he was able to communicate with them in Paiute, a language he knew. He learned that three white men had indeed appeared, claiming to have come down the Grand Canyon. The Shiwits didn't believe it for a minute, since no one had ever done such a thing. Still, they directed the strangers to a nearby spring. Soon afterward they heard from neighbors that three miners had killed an Indian woman in the area. Believing that Powell's men were the ones, they laid an ambush and shot them full of arrows.

"What did you do when they told you this?!" asked Fred, horror-struck.

"Oh, about then it was getting dark," said the Major, "so Hamblin and I bedded down for the night."

"With the Indians who murdered your men!?"

"Certainly."

But at this point, they could hear the roar of rapids ahead....

July 13, 1871

By now the explorers were many miles below Lodore, and the Major had gone ahead with an advance party of Jones, Hillers, and Cap in the *Emma Dean*. Cap took Fred's place, since the Major wanted another old army hand in case of trouble. The plan was to boat down to where the Uinta River joined the Green, stow the *Emma Dean*, and walk forty miles to the Ute Indian agency, which Powell had visited on the earlier voyage. This was to be the first supply point, and the Major wanted to get there as soon as possible to check on the provisioning effort being organized for him by Hamblin. He was also desperate for news from Emma.

Left in charge of the two remaining boats, Prof was traveling at a

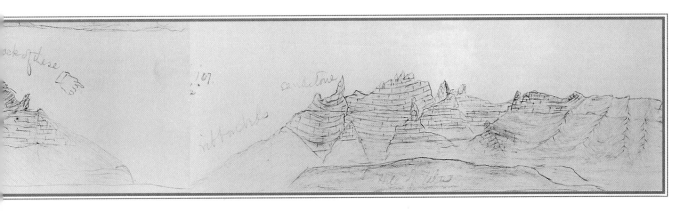

slower pace—mapping, sketching, photographing, and geologizing along the way. His group would catch up with the *Emma Dean* at the Uinta, where they would resupply and repair the boats. It was a sensible plan, but Fred and some of the others were troubled by it. They thought it a terrible idea to split up the expedition. That was a recipe for disaster! Around the campfire one night, Fred brought up every awful fate that might have befallen the advance party. Most of these involved arrows and tomahawks.

In fact, he was most upset about being replaced by Cap. He dearly wished that he could be sharing the danger—whatever it was.

A portion of Fred's continuous sketch of the river's left wall. This ten-mile segment extends from Whirlpool Canyon to Split Mountain Canyon, a distance the party covered from July 5–9, 1871. Fred includes notes about the type and age of rocks and the general geography.

CHAPTER VIII
Facing Starvation

July 29, 1871

"They can't find the Dirty Devil," Prof announced grimly.

"It's a slippery devil, ain't it?" quipped Hillers.

"Has to be if Old Jacob can't find it," mused Jones.

The explorers had reunited at the junction of the Uinta without arrows in the back, grizzlies at the throat, or drowned men in the rapids. They were busy restocking and patching their boats from the cache of supplies sent from the Ute agency. Meanwhile, the Major was on a side trip taking him first to the agency, then to Salt Lake City to check on Emma (who was reported sick), and then to southern Utah with Hamblin and some of his men to try to find the elusive spot for the next resupply: a muddy, smelly tributary of the Colorado called the Dirty Devil that was 300 miles downstream. The previous summer Powell and Hamblin had decided that a pack train could find its way overland to the Dirty Devil and down its canyon to the Colorado. But so far this had proved impossible, which was not a word in the vocabulary of either the Major or Old Jacob.

While the Major searched for the lost river, Prof's orders were to take the men and boats beyond Desolation and Coal canyons, about halfway to the Dirty Devil, to the crossing of the Old Spanish Trail, which led from Santa Fe to Los Angeles. There, the Major would try to rejoin them by September 3. If he didn't, Prof was to keep going on the assumption that Powell would show up at the Dirty Devil with a pack train later that month. In fact, Prof would not know until it was too late whether supplies or starvation awaited him, since the Major could die alone in the wilderness and leave the expedition stranded. The uncertainty made Prof as anxious as anything he'd experienced during the war.

The explorers at a borrowed cabin near the junction of the Uinta and Green rivers, August 4, 1871. Left to right: Fred (with spyglass), Hillers, Prof, Beaman, Clem, Steward, Andy, and Cap.

But the men were blissfully unconcerned. They had just averted another kind of starvation: lack of news. Along with the goods from the Ute agency had come mail, including hometown papers with articles written by some of the crewmen themselves. These were eagerly read aloud—and eagerly criticized.

"Why, Clem, how could you write such stuff?" objected Hillers to a breathless account in the Chicago *Tribune* that listed Clement Powell as author.

Clem tried to explain that the story, which featured wild cowboys and stampedes in Brown's Park, was either the work of his brother, who concocted the piece based on Clem's letters, or Richardson, who must be

*Douglas Boy and
his bride,
August 1, 1871.*

back in Illinois spreading tales about the trip. Anyway, said Clem, the
paper was probably eager to print a story by someone named Powell no
matter what the source.

But the campfire critics wouldn't buy it. "Naw," groused a skeptic,
"Richardson would never write that. He probably figures we're all
dead."

Jones's article fared better, being judged *bueno* ("good"). Fred's con-
tribution to the Buffalo *Courier* also met with approval, although someone

urged that he give more "color" to his writing next time. "But don't paint up the facts like that yarn spinner Clem."

August 5, 1871

For some weeks two Indians had been shadowing the expedition. They had appeared a few days after the Major split up the party above the Uinta, and they popped up here and there along the river. The young man and woman were Utes from Colorado Territory. They had run away together and were eluding the woman's fiancé.

The young man called himself Douglas Boy after his father, Chief Douglas. Prof's party made his acquaintance when he rode in fearlessly on the morning of July 13, signaling that he wanted food. After eating, he brought in the young woman. Later that day, Prof's men ferried the couple across the river by boat, while their horses swam. The pair probably went on to the Ute agency to get what food they could, before showing up again two weeks later farther downstream requesting another meal. They appeared one last time on August 5 near Desolation Canyon, but this time they were well provisioned with a deer, a portion of which they traded with the men for sugar.

These were the first Indians that Fred had ever seen, outside of medicine shows, train stations, and other city settings. They surprised him by being human in every way, down to their Romeo and Juliet predicament. He was bold, she was shy, and they were clearly in love. It was an old familiar story. But they had more on their minds than romance, for they and their people had become outcasts in their own country.

The Utes once lived throughout Utah, Colorado, and northern New Mexico. By the 1860s, they were hemmed into reservations on a fraction of their ancestral lands. No longer free to use their traditional hunting grounds, they were now chronically short of food. The reservation agencies operated by the United States government were supposed to give them provisions and teach them farming, but the supplies were inadequate and the agricultural methods impractical.

To Powell's men, the river and the surrounding territory seemed wild

Dellenbaugh Butte, depicted in a drawing by Fred and a photo by Beaman, September 4, 1871.

and unconquered. To the people who had occupied it for centuries, it seemed changed beyond comprehension. A Ute leader named Ouray, whom Douglas Boy probably knew, explained:

> *Long time ago, Utes always had plenty. On the*
> *prairie, antelope and buffalo, so many Ouray can't*
> *count. In the mountains, deer and bear everywhere.*
> *In the streams, trout, duck, beaver, everything....*
> *White man came, and now Utes go hungry....*

August 14, 1871

Andy fixed the bread for the midday meal while insisting that he did *not* laugh that morning when Clem fell into the river during a tricky letdown. All the men were soaked from the job, and most were sitting around in their underwear while their clothes dried in the sun. Fred was singing "Put Me in My Little Bed" and beating time with a stick, which pitched sand onto Cap, who complained sourly. Hillers lay comatose, too tired even to undress. Prof was down inspecting the next stretch of rapids with Jones, who offered nonstop advice on the best way to run it. Meanwhile, Beaman was making a photograph of the spot, which someone suggested calling Fretwater Falls. Amused by the entire spectacle, Steward was writing in his diary: "Here we are...presenting a scene more grotesque than beautiful."

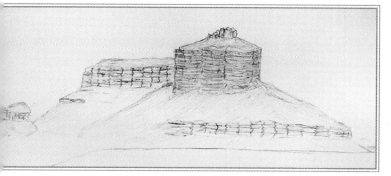 

August 26–29, 1871

Many fretful experiences later, Prof's men arrived at the crossing of the Old Spanish Trail. On their third day of waiting they heard three rapid shots. The Major's signal! Fred and Clem went to investigate, taking their rifles in case he was in trouble. Fortunately, he wasn't.

The Major reported no luck reaching the mouth of the Dirty Devil River. He and Hamblin had divided forces and approached it from two different directions—or so they thought. The Major gave up when his Indian guides abandoned him. The party under Old Jacob found what seemed to be the right river and followed its canyon for many miles, but it became increasingly impassable, so they gave up, too. Now Powell was resorting to the backup plan of bringing supplies down the Old Spanish Trail—as much as he, two Mormon guides, and a couple of pack animals could carry, which amounted to only a few bags of flour, some sugar, and dried meat. It was barely enough to last until the end of Monument Canyon, another 300 miles distant, where a little-used trail at a place called the Crossing of the Fathers offered the next resupply opportunity. The crossing was named after Father Silvestre Vélez de Escalante and his fellow missionaries, who forded the river at that spot during an overland expedition in 1776. The Major considered it a good place to halt for the season. From there, they could head overland to winter headquarters at Kanab, Utah, where Nellie, Emma, and, if all went well, a new baby would join them.

September 2–4, 1871

Back in his chair aboard the *Emma Dean,* the Major was grateful to be on the river again, especially since conditions allowed for a few days of relaxed boating, including more reading aloud. One day Fred remarked that a massive butte ahead resembled an art gallery. Powell announced, "Then we shall name it after our artist." And it was recorded on the charts as Dellenbaugh Butte.

September 13, 1871

The days were growing shorter, and supper was increasingly held by firelight. This night Andy intended to prepare a treat of stewed dried apples, since it was Fred's eighteenth birthday. Given the dwindling rations, it would constitute an extravagant feast. But the sheer walls of Stillwater Canyon offered few camping places, and by the time the explorers found a patch of level shoreline it was too late to celebrate.

Shinumo picture writing recorded by Fred near the Grand Canyon in 1872. Such mysterious carvings were found all along the Green and Colorado rivers.

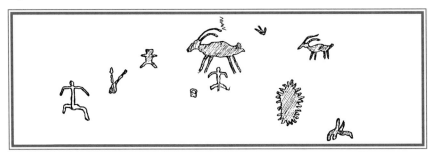

September 14, 1871

The Major and Prof took a field trip to hunt for fossils and ended up finding ancient cliff dwellings. It was remarkable evidence that people once lived a settled life in these wild canyons. The Major had discovered similar stone houses in the Grand Canyon during his first voyage, and he later asked local Indians what they knew about the long-vanished residents. Some told him that the gods destroyed the people because they knew too much. But their pottery, tools, and discarded corncobs showed that they certainly knew how to survive in a place where survival for the Powell party was still in doubt.

Around the campfire that evening, Powell talked about these ancient people. He called them the Shinumos, meaning "We the Wise," because of their obvious skill in agriculture, building, crafts, and a strange kind of picture writing. Perhaps they were part of a great civilization that once existed in the valleys of the Colorado.

"Perhaps," he went on, "they once sat around a fire at this very spot and talked about what lay at the end of this great river." He scratched his beard. "Perhaps they knew the legend that I heard last year in a Paiute village."

"What legend?" asked several listeners at once.

Powell began: "Long ago there was a great chief who mourned the death of his wife. The god Tavwoats came to him and said that he should not be sad, because his wife was in a happier land. The god promised to take the chief there, if, upon his return, he would cease to mourn. The great chief agreed. Then Tavwoats made a trail through the mountains to that happy land in the Far West. This trail was the canyon of the Colorado. Tavwoats led the chief down the trail to see his wife. When they returned, the god made him promise that he would tell no one of the path. Then Tavwoats rolled a mighty river into the canyon—a mad, raging stream, that should engulf anyone who might attempt to enter."

September 15, 1871

Inspired by the Major, Fred, Clem, and Steward rose at dawn and climbed up to the Indian ruins to explore. After breakfast some of the others came up as well, and it was early afternoon before everyone was back on the river—heading toward Tavwoats' forbidden path.

The canyon was narrow and steep, but the current was gentle and the rapids nonexistent. Clem remarked that it was the prettiest place they had yet been. Around four o'clock they rounded a promontory, and suddenly they faced another river of almost equal size. It was the Grand, flowing out of the Rocky Mountains in Colorado Territory. For 540 miles they had floated down the Green River, dropping 2,200 feet in altitude since departing Green River City. Here, the Green finally joined forces with the Grand. The current doubled in volume, although the dimensions of the river hardly changed. Already the explorers could sense the water surging within these confines. This was the Colorado.

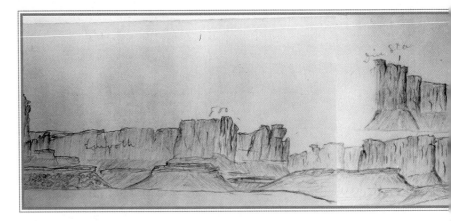

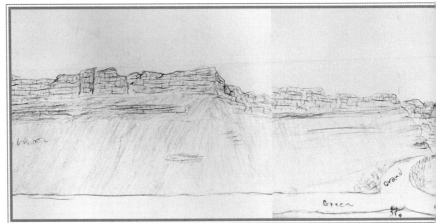

September 16–19, 1871

Here they stopped for several days. The Major wanted to map the area, and he and the others fanned out to explore and make observations. One morning he led a group, including Fred, up the western wall of the canyon. They made their way to a country that was astonishing to behold. As far as the eye could see were fantastically carved pinnacles, buttes, towers, columns, domes, pyramids, and every other shape that nature could sculpt out of stone. Powell had found the spectacle the previous day and said that he would name it Sinav-to-weap, which he explained was the Ute word for "Ghost Land." Beaman, who was setting up his camera, misheard it as *"God's* Land."

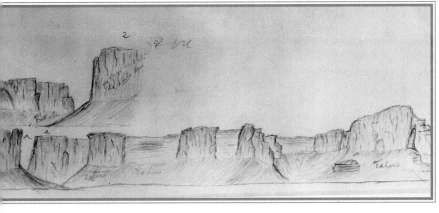

Winding through Labyrinth Canyon, below Dellenbaugh Butte—sketched by Fred on September 11, 1871.

The Colorado begins. Fred's drawing of the junction of the Green and Grand rivers, September 15, 1871.

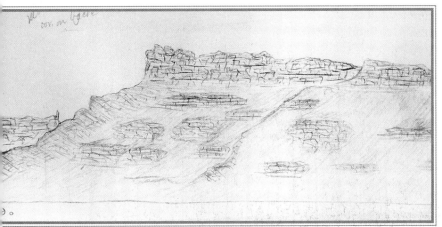

"Major," he protested, "it's no refuge for any of God's creatures—neither bird of the air nor beast of the field." Indeed, there was scarcely a plant to be seen.

Around the time of the Major's first voyage, a Western newspaper editor announced that he had laid out an entire city at the junction of the Green and Grand before being run off by Indians. The man probably thought that a city like St. Louis, which was located near the junction of the Missouri and Mississippi, would inevitably grow up at such a spot, and he wanted to stake a claim. Of course, there was no sign that he had ever been there, much less staked out a city. As Fred later wrote, "No more remote place existed at that time within the United States."

Preparing for departure, the explorers divided their remaining rations equally among the three boats so that an accident to one vessel would not doom them to starvation—at least not right away. Then on September 19, they started down the Colorado into Cataract Canyon— "dreaded Cataract Canyon," as Clem called it, based on his careful reading of Jack Sumner's diary from the first voyage.

September 21–29, 1871

"The water in the Colorado River is deeper and the rocks harder and sharper than in Green River; the current is far swifter," wrote Clem. He wasn't sure which was worse, running a rapid outright, or playing it safe with a letdown, in which case,

> *…the boat at times will be wedged in between the rocks while we are tugging and pulling away; suddenly away she will go, dragging us after her, holding on for dear life….'Tis a wonder that some of us have not had a leg or two broken. All of us wear horrible scars from our knees downward to remind us of the days when we made portages.*

Jones's painful reminder was a badly wrenched knee that was getting worse by the day. For Fred the worst part was the cold. At the bottom of the canyon, sunset came at three o'clock and with it a deepening chill that was quickly perceptible to the men in their drenched condition. Their teeth chattered uncontrollably and their lips turned blue. At night they sat by the fire for a long time, trying to restore their strength.

One of the strangest experiences in Cataract Canyon was the repeated rumble of distant thunder, which was not thunder at all but the sound of boulders being rolled underwater by the fierce current. Fred often saw huge rocks quaking with the crash of waves. Obviously, these were not places to be attempted in the boats, so the

Fred's sketch of Sinav-to-weap, or "Ghost Land," September 17, 1871.

men had to resort to frequent portages, significantly slowing their progress.

At the end of the canyon, they found cliffs riddled with caves. Fred, Cap, and Steward discovered ancient pottery and corncobs in the larger shelters, as well as scorpions. One of these crawled into Andy's shoe and stung him on the foot. The burning pain soon went away, but numbness set in, and Andy began to weaken.

September 30, 1871

They stopped at the mouth of the Dirty Devil. Each man was down to three small pieces of bacon, a fist-size piece of bread, and coffee with a little sugar for each meal. Supply wagons—had they managed to get through—would have been barely in time even here. But there were another 150 miles to go. The Major was willing to skip the scientific work to reach the Crossing of the Fathers as soon as possible. But he wanted to make up the lost data later, so he had the *Cañonita* stashed under a ledge so that some of the men could return and explore the river in detail the next spring. Heavily overloaded, the two remaining boats and ten explorers set forth on the final stretch.

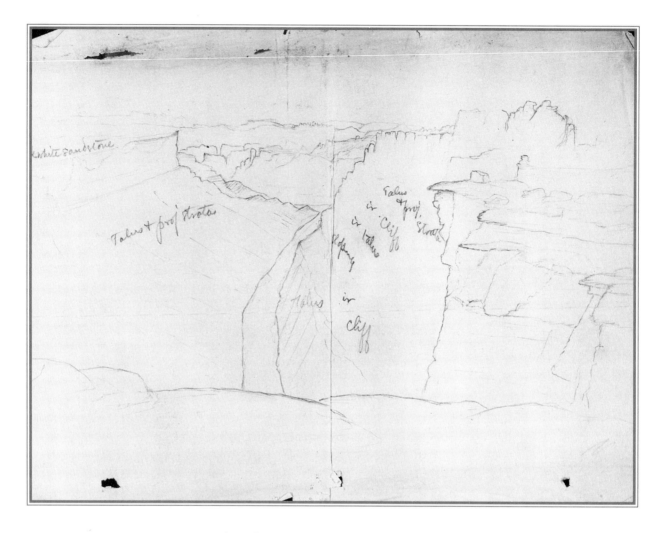

Clambering up the cliffs
on the river's right bank,
Fred made this sketch of
the beginnings of the
Colorado and start of
Cataract Canyon,
September 16, 1871.

October 1–5, 1871

They were in open country for a few miles before entering a new canyon
and a new set of rapids, though most of these were easily run, even in the
weighed-down boats. They passed beautiful caverns fringed with flowers and ferns. One of these was the Music Temple, a vast natural chamber
with magical acoustics, where Powell's first expedition had camped for a
day. The second expedition had no time to linger, but they stayed long
enough to find the carved names of three men from the earlier party —
the three, it happened, who were later killed by Indians.

Though feverish from the scorpion sting, Andy was making the rations last. He used the remaining bits of bacon as bait to catch some small fish. Even so, everyone knew that their condition was perilous and that any setback—a wrecked boat, a bout of bad weather—could spell doom.

October 6, 1871

Captain Dodds, head of the Ute agency on the Uinta, had been told to meet the Powell party at the Crossing of the Fathers with supplies by

September 25. After arriving early and waiting two weeks, he and his helpers were on the verge of giving up and leaving. Then a couple of boats with thin, ragged-looking men came into view. They were a sickly crew. Jones was crippled from his knee injury. Andy was pale and listless from the scorpion sting. Cap, who had been shot through the lung in the war, was feeling the effects of his old wound. Steward was collapsed from exhaustion, and Clem and Beaman nearly so. Prof and the Major were haggard and irritable. Hillers was far less spirited than usual. They had only two days of food left.

Fred, though, seemed barely affected, as if he were living off the taste of raw adventure itself. Soon after landing, he was learning how to pan for gold from one of Dodds's helpers, a prospector named Bonnemort.

CHAPTER IX
Kanab and the Unknown Country

December 25, 1871

Fred sat in a corner of the little stone hut that served as schoolhouse, temple, city hall, and dance hall for the thriving Mormon community of Kanab. Comprised of about forty families, the town had been founded a year earlier at the foot of the Vermilion Cliffs in southern Utah, roughly two days' ride west of the Colorado. The Powell party was camped in winter quarters nearby, joined by Nellie, Emma, and a healthy new baby—Mary Dean Powell, already fifteen weeks old.

On this night, Fred, Andy, Cap, Clem, Beaman, and Hillers were attending the town's Christmas dance. Lyman Hamblin, a son of Old Jacob, was playing the fiddle to shouts of "Ladies, change!" "Gentlemen, forward!" and other calls that turned the crowded, dimly lit room into a spectacle of shadowy, prancing forms. Too shy to take part, Fred watched from the sidelines along with most of his colleagues. Only the suave New Yorker Beaman was out on the floor, the others having been refused dances by the discriminating Kanab ladies.

The women had the pick of the territory for the evening, since quite a few strangers were in town. Mostly they were hunters, miners, and trappers, driven from the wilderness by the bad winter weather. Only the sober showed up at the dance, but even they had trouble getting partners, so Powell's men and the mountain men fell to talking to each other.

"Found any gold?" a toothless old-timer asked the explorers, by way of making conversation.

"Wouldn't be here if we had," said Clem, with faultless frontier logic.

"Maybe not," allowed the old-timer. Then he added, "Don't mind

Wanted! John D. Lee.

telling you that we"—he nodded to another man—"are doing a little prospecting down on the Colorado."

"Really?" said Clem a little suspiciously. Miners didn't usually tell you what they were doing.

"Thought you fellows might give us some suggestions," the old-timer went on. "Hear you know the river."

"That we do, at least as far as the Paria," said Clem. The Paria was a tributary thirty-five miles below the Crossing of the Fathers. Powell and his men had stashed the *Emma Dean* and the *Nellie Powell* there before trekking overland to Kanab.

"Ever run into a man by the name of John Doyle?" the old-timer continued.

At this point Cap, who considered himself the senior man of the Powell group, broke in. "We haven't run into much of anybody. Why do you ask?"

"He's got a price on his head—ten thousand dollars. You might say he's what we're prospecting for."

"Oh, ho!" joined in Andy. "Who did he kill?"

"Reckon he killed about a hundred and twenty men, women, and children. That's all!"

Sitting nearby, Fred listened intently as the old-timer talked on. It developed that John Doyle was an alias for none other than John D. Lee. He was the Mormon leader who was allegedly responsible for the massacre of California-bound settlers in the incident that was mentioned by the woman on the train when Fred was traveling to Chicago to meet the Major. The old-timer suspected that Lee was hiding out near the Colorado. On the other hand, Lee was also rumored to be holed up just outside of Kanab.

Getting nowhere with Powell's men, the old-timer surveyed the crowd of dancers and grumbled, "Tell you one thing. Every Mormon in this room knows where Lee is, but just ain't saying."

January 15, 1872

"Yes, I know John D. Lee very well," said Old Jacob. "Very well."

Having raised the subject, Prof leaned forward in his chair to hear more. So did Fred and Jones. The three were dining with Old Jacob while in Kanab getting ready for a field trip.

"Back in fifty-seven," Hamblin continued, "Lee was a major in our militia. At that time our church was very hard-pressed by your government—very hard-pressed. They were sending soldiers to invade us and depose our leaders...and perhaps kill us. We did not know what to expect. But we had been persecuted before in Missouri and many other places, and so we knew how to be prepared. That summer a rough party of immigrants passed through on their way to California. Many immigrants passed through back then, but we feared the worst from these, since they threatened us repeatedly and told us that soldiers were just behind them. When they got to Mountain Meadows on the Old Spanish Trail, they were attacked by the Paiutes, who also feared them. The immigrants repulsed the attack, and the Paiutes began a siege. Lee was on a mission nearby, and since the Paiutes were our allies, he came to take command of the situation."

Old Jacob breathed deeply and went on. "Some say the Paiutes did all the killing. Some say our own men were involved. Nobody will talk about it. All I know is that when I went to Mountain Meadows not many days after, I found a horrible scene. The slain numbered over one hundred men, women, and children. They had been buried in shallow graves, and at three places wolves had dug them up and left them strewn in every direction. At one place I saw nineteen wolves pulling out the bodies and eating the flesh...."

Prof was beginning to regret having brought up such painful memories. As soon as he could, he steered the conversation to another subject. But as they fell to talking about explorers in the old days, Old Jacob mentioned that Lieutenant Ives and his Colorado exploring party had come through not many months after the Mountain Meadows incident. These strangers, too, were greeted with deep suspicion. But this time they were let go with their lives.

As for the invasion the Mormons feared, it never amounted to much. The Mormons were left to themselves—although the United States government vowed to track down those responsible for the Mountain Meadows massacre.

February 1, 1872

One by one as the winter wore on, the members of the Second Powell Expedition were dropping away, worn down and played out. Richardson, of course, had been the first to go. Then Steward left in ill health in early November, shortly after the party arrived at the Paria. Now Cap, who was also ailing, had decided to settle down in Utah and was finishing up his maps for the Major.

Beaman, too, was departing. His plan was to strike out on his own and make pictures of the most spectacular scenery in the West, which he could then sell back east without having to split profits with the Major, which was the current arrangement. Clem, who had been serving as his assistant, was to take over as photographer.

After settling matters with Beaman, the Major set out for Salt Lake City with Emma and little Mary to catch the train to Washington, D.C. Powell's goal was to raise more money from Congress to continue and even extend the expedition. Meanwhile, Prof and the others were to map the area around Kanab as far south as the rim of the Grand Canyon, about forty miles away. In late spring they would head back to the mouth of the Dirty Devil, taking a route through a region called the Unknown Country. At the Dirty Devil one crew would retrieve the *Cañonita* and float down the Colorado to the Paria, where the other two boats were stowed. The other explorers—including the Major, who would have returned from the East by then—would travel overland and rendezvous with the *Cañonita* at the Paria. The three boats would then set forth toward the Grand Canyon on what promised to be the climactic adventure of the voyage.

May 25, 1872

Nellie wanted to go, too. She considered herself just as expert at outdoor life as her brother, the Major, and just as knowledgeable about nature as her husband, Prof. Her cousin Clem agreed. So did Fred, who had gotten to know her well since arriving in Kanab and considered her the most cheerful and resolute explorer of the whole company. For most of the spring, Nellie had joined the men on their wide-ranging field trips through southern Utah and northern Arizona. No one knew botany as well as she did, and no one added as many new plant specimens to the scientific treasures of the expedition. Even so, Prof decided that she had to stay behind while he and the others headed across the Unknown Country in search of the Dirty Devil—the elusive tributary that had defeated Old Jacob's attempts to pin it down the previous year.

Accompanying Prof were a mix of familiar faces and new recruits. There were the five remaining veterans: Fred, Hillers, Jones, Andy, and Clem. There were two Mormon settlers, Will Johnson and George Adair, who had signed on to replace Cap and Steward. There was a new photographer, James Fennemore, a Mormon from Salt Lake City. He was taking over from Clem, who couldn't get the hang of the skill despite hard months of trying (Clem would stay on as photographic assistant and general helper). There was Captain Dodds, head of the Ute agency on the Uinta, who had led the supply party to the Crossing of the Fathers the previous fall. Prior to that he had joined Old Jacob in the wild-goose chase for the mouth of the Dirty Devil. At that time they'd been unable to figure out which creek, stream, river, gully, or other tributary in the Unknown Country ended up where the Dirty Devil flowed into the Colorado. But Dodds now had his candidate.

May 26–June 22, 1872

Nine days of riding brought the men to a pretty river in a charming valley about seventy miles northeast of Kanab. "Yep, I've been here before," said Dodds. "This has gotta be the Dirty Devil. It starts here and heads east, which is where we want to be." They headed east, following the river.

Three days later, surveying the surrounding country from a high point, Prof shook his head. He pulled out his compass. "Look here, Dodds. This river has veered south. It's on a beeline for a point pretty far downstream from where we know the Dirty Devil comes in." He turned to his left and pointed to a mountain range about forty miles to the east. "See those peaks. The Dirty Devil intersects the Colorado just beyond them, on the other side. We're in the wrong valley."

"Well, what cussed river is this?" demanded Dodds.

Prof admitted that he didn't know a tributary of this size that entered the Colorado anywhere between the Dirty Devil and the Paria, although this one must. "Maybe we'll have to name it," he ventured.

The next day, the party backtracked to the headwaters of the mystery

*Prof scouting the
country, 1873.*

river, wondering what it was and where it went, although these questions would have to wait. At this point, Prof decided to send Jones, Clem, and Adair back to Kanab to get more provisions, since the expedition was going to take far longer than planned. The three were to bring the supplies to the same spot in twelve days. Meanwhile, Prof would head north with the others to search for a route to the Dirty Devil Mountains, the range he had pointed out to Dodds. From there they ought to be able to find the Dirty Devil River and the *Cañonita*. He would dispatch a crew down the Colorado in the boat, while he and the rest returned to the headwaters of the mystery river to rendezvous with the resupply party.

Five days later, Prof and his men were still trying to reach the mountain range. They had been traveling across a lushly forested plateau, but now this pleasant landscape veered northwest, while they needed to head east. Twenty-five miles away they could see the Dirty Devil Mountains. In between lay a rugged desert. Searching for a path that the Indians may have made into this arid wilderness, Prof sent Fred and Johnson down a gully leading off the plateau. They returned, reporting an old trail with signs of recent use. Prof decided to take it.

Two days down this path, a barking dog proclaimed that someone was nearby. It was an encampment of Utes, who were frightened at first but soon turned friendly. Using signs and words, the chief asked if the explorers had any gunpowder to trade. All Prof and his men had were cartridges, which wouldn't work in the tribe's old muzzle loaders. Using similar methods of communication, Prof asked if any of the Indians would serve as guides to the Dirty Devil Mountains. None volunteered, but the chief gave minutely detailed directions. Unfortunately, Prof was unable to follow them.

After a night's sleep near the Indian camp, the explorers pressed on and soon got lost in a maze of canyons. Late the following day they climbed out and could see the Dirty Devil Mountains—closer than ever, fortunately. All the next day they followed a ridge above a network of deep ravines. By afternoon they were at the foot of the range, and by evening they were camped high on the slopes of one of the peaks.

The next morning Prof, Dodds, and Hillers started for the summit in order to make observations of the surrounding country. Assigned to climb an adjoining peak, Fred and Johnson had to turn back when a snow squall hit and Johnson gave out from cold and exhaustion. However, Prof's team made it to the top and could see the valley of the Dirty Devil River, cutting through the desert below and into the Colorado. The Dirty Devil was right where Prof had predicted—well to the north of the region where Old Jacob and Dodds had looked for it.

Another four days of climbing, backtracking, and canyon-hopping brought the weary explorers to the junction of the Dirty Devil and Colorado, exactly four weeks after leaving Kanab. The Unknown Country was unknown no more. And the *Cañonita* was right where they had left it.

June 23, 1872

The second season of river work could now begin. Prof assigned Fred, Hillers, Johnson, and Fennemore to take the *Cañonita* to the Paria, mapping and photographing as they went to make up for the rush through that section the previous fall. Meanwhile, Prof, Dodds, and Andy would return to the headwaters of the mystery river—in days rather than weeks this time, since they now knew the way. There they would meet up with Jones, Clem, Adair, and the wagonload of supplies. After more exploring in the area, the six would return to Kanab, presumably to find the Major taking care of last-minute arrangements for the coming journey into the Grand Canyon. Everyone would then pack up and head for the Paria, meeting up with the *Cañonita* crew in about three weeks. In case of delay, Prof promised to send a couple of men with provisions to be waiting when Fred's group arrived.

June 26–July 4, 1872

After repairing and repainting the *Cañonita*, Fred's group set off—with

Johnson, Fred, and Hillers repairing the Cañonita *at the mouth of the Dirty Devil River, June 1872.*

Fred at the helm commanding the expedition, Hillers and Johnson rowing, and Fennemore sitting on deck.

Since Fred and Hillers had covered this stretch of river the previous fall, the voyage was more of an excursion for them than an expedition, especially since the river was higher now and what rapids there were posed few problems. But on shore there was still much to do, particularly for Fennemore as photographer and Hillers as his assistant. Johnson's job was to set up camp. Fred kept busy sketching, mapping, and cooking. On the Fourth of July, he made a lemon cake and a peach pie. His usual meal was bread, which he baked in a skillet, and coffee.

July 7, 1872

Alerted by Prof to keep an eye out for the mystery river, they spotted it. No one would have guessed that this shallow, narrow tributary of the Colorado was a major river—perhaps the last to be discovered in the United States. It had misled Old Jacob and Dodds the previous year, when they sent the Major's pack train of supplies into its impassable canyons, convinced that it was the Dirty Devil. It had misled the Major himself—twice, when on both of his expeditions he sailed right past without realizing it was the key to the Unknown Country, the last major unmapped region of the West. Not until Prof's recent trek did anyone recognize that this was a completely new river. Prof had decided to name it the Escalante, after Father de Escalante of the crossing downstream.

July 8–13, 1872

Fred and his crew arrived at the cavern Powell called the Music Temple—a magnificent place to be stranded for two days of hard rain. Fred used part of the time to carve his name and Hillers' alongside those of the three murdered explorers from the first expedition.

On July 12, they reached the Crossing of the Fathers, where they dug up some photographic supplies that had been left the previous year. They had much greater need of food but were confident of resupply

THE
WILD
COLORADO

when they reached the Paria, probably the next day. Their brief mission was nearly over, and they had done a thorough job of documenting this section of the river.

On July 13, they landed at the Paria, pulling up next to the *Emma Dean*, which had been moved from its storage place. Presumably some of the other men were already there, although they were nowhere to be seen. Fred gave the usual signal—three rapid shots fired in the air. No reply. Investigating further, he noticed that since the fall a rough-looking cabin had been built nearby. As he and the others approached it, they saw an old man standing outside, watching them. Johnson recognized him—it was a fellow Mormon. "That's John D. Lee," he whispered.

CHAPTER X
Lonely Dell

Moments later

The old man received the visitors politely, if a little suspiciously. "Welcome to Lonely Dell," he said, and shook hands all around. He immediately invited them to come to his cabin for supper that evening.

While setting up camp near the boats, Johnson told Fred that he wanted to go back to Kanab as soon as possible. His health, he said, would not permit a voyage through the Grand Canyon. Fred had already concluded the same thing, but he also wondered if Lee's presence had anything to do with this sudden announcement.

That evening

Sitting down with his guests, the old man wasted no time. He stared at Fred, whom he judged to be in charge, and said, "Perhaps you have heard who I am?"

Fred swallowed hard and decided to be just as direct. "Some people say you're John D. Lee."

The old man was silent for a moment, then said very deliberately, "I have come to Lonely Dell so that I will not be taken. Whoever tries will feel hot lead from my seven-shooter and my seventeen-shooting rifle." He nodded to a corner where Fred could see the firearms, presided over by one of Lee's rugged-looking wives. Like many Mormon men, Lee had several companions in marriage—eighteen, according to some reports, although only two were present.

Lee went on. "I will not betray those who did the act through their great zeal in serving our church. They were provoked to it by the worst set of immigrants who ever crossed the plains. Those people had two bulls which they named after our leaders and whipped them through our towns, yelling and singing, cursing and swearing to make your hair stand on end. They boasted that they killed our brethren when we were persecuted in Missouri—killed us and threw our bodies down a well. I do not know if they were telling the truth or lying just to torment us, but either way they brought vengeance on themselves!"

Lee looked down and began to sob. "I tried to stop it....When we held council at Mountain Meadows and voted to kill them, I wept like a child and would not consent to have anything to do with it....I pleaded for the women and children's lives. The Indians called me *Yauguts*—crybaby—and they still do."

He wiped his eyes. "But it cannot be helped now. Vengeance has been done. Our blood was shed in great streams in Missouri, and if at last some of us did rise up and smite our enemies, I won't consent to give them up. It suits many people to blame me, and drive me from my farms and houses to this Lonely Dell. But I will never be taken. You may tell your friends that it would be useless to try." He nodded again at his arsenal. "I could defy an army from these rocks."

"We don't want to take you," blurted Fred. "We're explorers." As soon as he said it, he realized it might sound suspiciously like "bounty hunters" to the trigger-happy old man.

But Lee had a different response: "I'm an explorer myself."

July 14—24, 1872

Few people knew as much about Mormon country as John D. Lee. He had explored throughout the region since arriving with the first Mormon immigrants twenty-five years before, and he admired and understood men who came with a thirst for knowledge about an unknown place. On the other hand, he also understood men who came with a thirst for a ten-thousand-dollar reward, and he knew how one thirst could be overwhelmed by the other. So he stayed on his guard.

Soon he had even more explorers to keep track of, for on July 15, Prof's resupply party—Clem and Andy—showed up with a wagonload of provisions. They reported that the Major had not yet returned from the East, though he was expected in Kanab any day.

Two versions of the Mountain Meadows massacre. Top: Mormon settlers do the deed. Bottom: Paiute Indians are mostly to blame.

Johnson left as announced, and Powell's men at Lonely Dell now numbered five. Fennemore, who had been sick on and off since joining the expedition, was growing worse. Lee judged him entirely unfit for an explorer's life and eventually moved him into his cabin. Fred, Hillers,

Andy, and Clem spent a few days overhauling their boats and helping Lee improve his property, mainly by working on his irrigation projects. Unfortunately, at one point their good deeds were washed away by a flash flood.

On July 24, Lee invited the men to celebrate the silver anniversary of Mormon settlement in Utah. A fine dinner of summer vegetables was prepared for the occasion, and Lee entertained his guests with jokes, card games, songs, and sermons. Clem, who had already penciled "Think Lee is a little crazy" in his diary, saw no reason to change his opinion, though he did have a wonderful time. After describing Lee's frontier hospitality, he concluded the day's entry: "Reached camp after dark, wondering why the Maj. & Prof don't come."

July 26, 1872

Sweltering in 110-degree heat, Fred scratched the page of his diary with a pencil that seemed about to melt—or catch fire: "Same monotonous camp life. So hot that one can scarcely move, but after all there is nothing to move for. Our camp surroundings are sand and rocks and before us flows the Colorado in all its majesty just at present thick with red mud. We gaze down the canyon and wonder if they will ever come, if we will ever get started and if we do how long we will dally in the Grand Canyon. Wonder if they have heard anything of the Major at Kanab or anywhere else, etc., etc."

July 27, 1872

Fred: "Around camp as usual today with nothing to do. Sat under the boat shelter all day today."

July 30, 1872

Clem: "Fred, Jack and I fired at a mark in the evening."

July 31, 1872

Fred: "Same routine."

August 1, 1872

Fred: "We wonder why some one don't come."

August 2, 1872

Clem: "I cut Fred's and Jack's hair and Fred cut mine in return. Some of Lee's folks coming in from Kanab said that the Maj. had not come in up to Monday last."

August 3, 1872

Clem: "We spent the days studying, reading, swimming, sleeping, eating, etc."

August 4–12, 1872

Impatient to know what was holding up the expedition, the group finally decided that someone should go to Kanab. Clem volunteered, but the others were secretly worried he would get lost. Insisting that it was only fair to share the risk by drawing straws, they arranged for Fred to win the honor. He rode out late in the day on August 4, after first promising Lee that there was no trap in the works, for the abrupt departure looked suspicious to the old man. Five days later, Fred returned with Jones, Lyman Hamblin, and another wagon of supplies. The Major's party was supposedly on its way, though Fred had not seen any sign of it.

On Fred's arrival, Lee immediately cornered him. He knew Old Jacob's son, Lyman—but who was the other man? Fred assured Lee that Jones was no bounty hunter and was trustworthy. Lee relaxed a bit, but he was also concerned about Lyman. It was well known that Old Jacob had condemned the Mountain Meadows affair, and Lee believed the son was just as prejudiced against him.

Three days later, Clem and the others were still biding their time: "Looking for the party all day long, reading, sleeping, talking, etc. Spent the evening pleasantly singing, etc."

CHAPTER XI
"The Sockdolager of the World"

August 13–15, 1872

On August 13—one month late—the Major finally arrived at Lonely Dell. He was accompanied by Prof, Nellie, Adair, an Indian guide, and Harvey De Motte, a professor at the Illinois college where Powell taught. De Motte was out west on a summer excursion. That evening he and Nellie joined Fred, Jones, and Hillers for a boat ride.

Out on the water Nellie was charmed. "This is delightful! What makes the whirlpools?"

Experiencing the Colorado for the first time, De Motte explained: "The monstrous boulders beneath the waves, Mrs. Thompson, direct the current into spirals that cause these vigorous vortices. But never fear! We are safe. Our trusty helmsman, Jones, is a skilled pilot on these waters. And our oarsmen, Hillers and Dellenbaugh, can propel us out of any danger."

Enjoying the easy run, Fred could only smile.

Nellie went out the next day on a far rougher ride without De Motte. She returned begging Prof and the Major to let her join the expedition. But they refused, noting that the new recruits—Johnson, Fennemore, and Adair—had all dropped out of the Grand Canyon trip. Surely these experienced Westerners had made a realistic assessment of the hazards. Nellie countered that she was strong enough and quick enough. Furthermore she could do scientific work, identifying new species of plants in the canyons—something none of the men knew much about.

But the Major was adamant. Only his veterans would go. He, Jones, Hillers, and Fred would return to the *Emma Dean*. Prof, Andy, and Clem would man the *Cañonita*. The least seaworthy of the boats, the *Nellie Powell*, would be left behind at Lonely Dell for Lee to use as a ferry. As for the real Nellie—she, too, must stay behind.

Sobered by the dangers ahead, the men wrote last-minute letters and got other details in order. Nellie did what she could to help, repairing ragged clothing such as Andy's patched and repatched canvas coat, which had become a joke around camp. The Major settled accounts with Lee and others for their services, and arranged for Adair to resupply the expedition at Kanab Wash, in the depths of the Grand Canyon, by September 4.

On August 15, Nellie, Fennemore, Hamblin, Adair, and De Motte departed, leaving the explorers to their final preparations.

August 17, 1872

Since leaving Green River City fifteen months earlier, the Second Powell Expedition had navigated more than 700 river-miles, dropping almost 3,000 feet in elevation. They had roughly as far to go in both mileage and altitude to reach the mouth of the Colorado, if indeed that was their destination. As usual, no one was quite sure what the Major was planning.

In any case, the most dangerous part of the trip lay directly ahead: Marble Canyon and then the Grand Canyon, the wildest ride of all.

Fortunately, the men were completely at home in their well-practiced roles, ready to take on whatever the river dished out. The only difference in duties was that Hillers was now photographer, having taken over from Fennemore. Prof had been impressed with Hillers' knack with a camera when he sometimes filled in for the ailing Fennemore during the trip to the Unknown Country. As Prof explained to Powell, Hillers would "work harder and select better, more characteristic and artistic views" than his predecessors. Indeed, photographs were more important than ever, since Fred would no longer be making continuous sketches of the canyon walls. He would be far too busy at the oars for that.

"Started down Marble Canyon at about ten o'clock A.M.," wrote Clem in his diary. "The water is higher than usual and we soon come to our old friend, the rapids, running one after the other....Have not felt so tired in a long time."

THE
WILD
COLORADO

*View down Marble
Canyon, photographed
by Hillers on
August 21, 1872.*

August 18—20, 1872

The walls of Marble Canyon grew higher and the river narrower as the explorers ventured ever deeper into the somber chasm. Bands of rock that started out at water level gradually rose with the cliffs, exposing layers underneath and adding to the impression that they were descending into

the very earth—which, geologically, they were.

Taking pictures at every stop, Hillers had a setback when he discovered that water had seeped into his plate box and ruined most of his negatives. Prof took the blame, since he had failed to secure the rubber sack protecting the plates when he loaded the *Cañonita*.

Fred's sketch of Marble Canyon, looking the opposite direction from the facing photo. At the far bend of the river is a giant cavern.

August 21, 1872

Dawn was officially at six A.M., but the narrow canyon and high walls hid the sun until midmorning, cloaking the Colorado in a mysterious gloom. Soon after starting out in this half-light, the explorers neared a sharp turn in the river. Fred stared into the shadows and tried to imagine what was next.

"Major," he said, "what would you have done on the first trip if just beyond that bend you had come upon a fall like Niagara?"

Powell thought it over. "I don't know," he said finally.

Another Niagara was unlikely, to be sure. But it was easy for Fred to imagine that the canyon walls were about to blot out the sky as the river drilled a stupendous cavern directly into the earth itself, like the underground passages of the mythical Colorado. Rounding the bend, they came to a real cavern, cut into the limestone cliff just above the shoreline. They stopped to explore and take pictures. Powell guessed that the huge space would hold 50,000 people.

Continuing downstream, they encountered two of the biggest rapids they had yet seen. By midafternoon the sun was again behind the high walls. The explorers floated on in the early twilight until they came to a small, narrow tributary where sand had been washed down to form a beach. Hearing the roar of rapids ahead, Powell decided to pitch camp.

Clem recorded the scene:

> *At a gray dusk of evening, just after landing, camps wear their most picturesque garb. Maj. and Prof looking over maps and books; others spreading blankets or attending to other little duties. Andy preparing supper. The darkness increases, the campfire grows brighter. The stars come out one by one in the narrow rift of blue that seems so far away. Two boats, bruised and battered but still so graceful in outline and symmetry, swing idly at the bank. We*

*look at them with feelings of pride and trust; we look
to them to carry us safely to the outside world. We
gather around our meal and discuss the events of the
past day. Cigarettes are then made and lighted and
consumed. Silence overtakes us. The moonbeams are
creeping softly downwards. One by one the explorers
roll up in their blankets. The camp-fire dims out.
Danger, privation and toil are forgotten and our
thoughts are of our far-away homes. The moonbeams
are at the foot of the opposite cliff and we are lulled
to sleep by the roar of the rapids below us.*

August 22, 1872

The morning's rapids posed few problems, but after lunch the men were
swept into an adventure that seemed certain to end badly.

"By God, boys, we're gone!" exclaimed the Major as he saw a fear-
some drop ahead with white foam exploding above barely concealed
boulders. There was no chance to reach shore. The men gritted their teeth
expecting disaster. But the two craft slipped through the first section
miraculously, the rocks being farther below the surface than they
appeared. The Major led the boats through the rest of the run with shouts
of "Left! Right! Hard on the right! Steady! Hard on the left! *Hard on the
left!* H-A-R-D ON THE LEFT! Pull away strong!" When the boats had got
through at last, Powell confessed that he had no recollection of so severe
a stretch at the same point on the first trip. The water was higher now
than in '69, and therefore running faster and creating new danger spots.

During calmer moments, the explorers saw that the hemmed-in walls
of Marble Canyon were beginning to recede, revealing cliff upon cliff in
an increasingly breathtaking vista. By four o'clock they arrived at the
junction of the Little Colorado and its spectacular gorge, which merged
with the Colorado from the east. Below was what Powell termed "the
Sockdolager of the World," the "knockout punch" of all canyons: the
Grand Canyon.

The head of Jack Sumner's "perfect hell of waves" in the granite gorge of the Grand Canyon, August 29, 1872.

August 23–28, 1872

The party proceeded slowly and carefully, allowing time for mapping, photography, and rock collecting. At first the weather was oppressively hot. But by the twenty-eighth, a hard rain had set in, punctuated by severe hail. "Came pretty near freezing," noted Clem, who was recovering from a sprained back and felt terrible. The same day Hillers wrenched his back and was in even worse shape. He desperately needed a day or two to recover, but the expedition had to keep moving, since rations were once again getting tight. "If we can survive for the next two or three days," wrote Clem, "will be all right to the Kanab Wash, at least." That

was the spot where Adair and a couple of packers were due to meet them with provisions.

August 29, 1872

In the morning Hillers awoke nearly paralyzed. Fred rubbed his back with camphor, giving him relief enough to walk with the aid of an oar. He made his way along the shore to the foot of the next rapid, while Andy rowed first in the *Emma Dean,* then hiked back to repeat the run in the *Cañonita.*

With steep cliffs again hemming in the river, Hillers stiffly resumed his post. The party advanced into a gorge cut into solid granite—the oldest, deepest, hardest rock in the canyon. The formation guaranteed rough water wherever fallen rocks littered the river, which was often. Surveying the section immediately ahead, Fred thought it the most dreadful he had ever seen or hoped to see. This was the "perfect hell of waves" described in Jack Sumner's diary, which had caused so much nervousness back in Green River City. *Emma Dean* was first through. Waiting his turn in the *Cañonita*, Clem lost sight of his comrades and feared the worst. But after a brief moment he glimpsed "four human heads on top of the next wave, the boat nearly filled with water." After both crews completed the run, all agreed it was the fiercest yet—an award they were bestowing almost daily.

They let down around part of another section of rapids and camped on the bare granite in the midst of heavy rain. They were a mile deep in the earth…and the river was rising.

August 30, 1872

All the next day the rain kept up while the men continued the portage. By afternoon the *Emma Dean* and the *Cañonita* had gaping holes from being battered on the rocks. Drenched and exhausted, the men hauled the boats to a ledge for repairs. Before they could finish, the river had risen three feet. They hauled the boats still higher. Later, in darkness, they hauled them even higher—as high as they could—while the river continued to rise. Searching for firewood, Fred found driftwood a hundred feet up the canyon wall, a sign of how high the water could go. "'Tis an anxious night for us all," wrote Clem. "The party seems dead—nothing but work and danger, hard beds and worse food."

And rain…

August 31, 1872

…Still raining.

"A gloomy morning in a gloomier locality," wrote Fred after a miserable night. "Ate breakfast as quickly as possible so as to get out of our trap." The river had dropped slightly during the night but now was rising again. As the men lowered the *Emma Dean* into the torrent, she lurched and struck a sharp rock, driving a hole clean through the hull. Water began filling the middle cabin. For a moment the Major considered hauling her out again for repair, but he decided they couldn't afford to stay. "By God, we'll start!" he declared. "Load up!" Working like demons, the men threw in their gear, losing some of it to the river. They jammed a sack of flour against the leak—which hardly helped. Shoving off, they were already so waterlogged they could barely steer around an enormous rock fifty feet downstream.

Meanwhile, the other crew was scrambling to get the *Cañonita* loaded. They jettisoned unneeded items but also lost critical ones, including an oar. After shoving off, they were propelled straight for the big rock. Prof prayed they would strike only a glancing blow and bounce off in one piece. Miraculously, they were captured by an eddy and pushed backward, allowing them to row into the main current and get safely around the obstacle. Meeting at a protected cove a little downstream, both crews beached and began a new round of repairs, wondering how long they could keep cheating disaster and death.

That evening, after running another ten miles and ten rapids, Clem wrote wearily, "All of us are about used up." They were camped at a clear stream that Powell had given the hopeful name Bright Angel Creek. It was his way of balancing the evident bad luck of naming a feature upstream the Dirty Devil.

September 1, 1872

Recovered from his back injury, Hillers was taking as many pictures as ever. But now Jones was ill. This may have led to an accident in which he lost his balance and fell overboard into a rapid. He managed to catch hold of the *Emma Dean,* but he nearly capsized it trying to get back in. The *Cañonita* was no luckier, getting a hole knocked through the hull, which required yet another repair stop.

And it was still raining…

Repair stop on September 1, 1872. The Cañonita is upended to patch a hole. Fred is at the extreme left. The other men are probably Andy, Jones, and Prof, whose head is just above the left foreground boulder.

September 2, 1872

The Major guessed that the Colorado was eight to ten feet higher than it had been in 1869, making the boats travel at locomotive speed. "High water is a great labor-saving institution," joked Clem, "as long as one is right side up." On this day they were—running twenty rapids and more than fifteen miles without mishap. Even the weather cooperated, with the nearly constant rains starting to let up. Kanab Wash could not come too soon, however, since the dried beef was spoiled and infested with inch-long worms, which gave it "a queer taste" to Fred. Andy did what he could to make it palatable. He had to—there was little else to eat.

Late in the day they came to an imposing stretch of rapids that Hillers termed "busters." Prof doubted that they could be run at all, judging them absolutely the worst yet. But the Major disagreed, announcing they would attack the spot head-on the next morning.

September 3, 1872

"Oh, ho, boys!" intoned the Major just after dawn to rouse his exhausted sleepers. Prof and Andy were already stirring, but the others had not yet thrown off their blankets.

Once up, fatigue affected each of them differently. Hillers sang more quietly than usual. Jones was grimmer, more like the school principal he formerly was. Clem was more irritable, ready for the expedition to end but determined not to give up. Andy seemed resigned to whatever happened. Prof was himself—fretful about the day's plan and trying to convince the Major to change it. For his part, the Major seemed positively happy to be risking all. And Fred was like a dazed boxer, battered but still punching—not yet laid low by the Sockdolager of the World.

At eight A.M. they shoved off. The high water quickly carried them into a gentle rapid that preceded the "busters." Once through, the Major rose from his chair, gripped the arm to steady himself, and stared at the ordeal ahead. Seeing it clearly for the first time, he suddenly had second thoughts. "Hard left, boys! HARD LEFT FOR THE SHORE!" But it was too late. The *Emma Dean* made a wild leap into the mad water; the *Cañonita* was not far behind.

Curling waves rolled one after another over the two boats, swamping the cockpits and making steering nearly impossible. On the boats rushed at the mercy of a frenzied, unforgiving river, like wood chips sweeping over Niagara. When it seemed that the worst was over, Fred and Hillers let go of their oars and started bailing for life. Then a powerful whirlpool swung them around, just as the biggest wave of all lifted them up...up...up...and over. Men and equipment spilled into the seething vortex. The Major disappeared. Grasping for the boat, Hillers was knocked sideways by an attached oar and fell headlong after the Major.

Holding the upended boat, Fred was blinded by his hat pasted over his eyes. Pulling it free, he found he was alone. The Major, Hillers, Jones, the crew of the *Cañonita*—all were gone. And he was rushing down a savage river toward a dark bend....

September 4, 1872

On the day of the Major's appointed arrival at Kanab Wash, Adair and two helpers stood on the beach gazing upriver at something floating their way. The object drifted closer. The men squinted hard to see it. As if to satisfy their curiosity, it veered toward shore and eventually caught on a rock. Adair waded out to investigate and found it was an old canvas coat, heavily patched. "It's Andy Hattan's," he told the others. They looked at him. "Powell's cook," he explained.

CHAPTER XII
Final Mission

September 3–7, 1872

Fred was struggling to pull himself onto the hull of the capsized *Emma Dean* when he caught sight of a pair of hands gripping the other end. It was Jones! A moment later, the Major and Hillers miraculously shot from the mouth of the whirlpool, as if from the barrel of a cannon. Flailing and gasping, they reached out and grabbed the boat. As the four survivors started to turn the *Emma Dean* over, another miracle occurred as the *Cañonita* sped by, right side up with its crew intact. Both boats made their way to a beach about a mile and a half downstream, where the badly shaken explorers unloaded and dried off. Luckily, the scare was worse than the damage.

At this point they were still thirty-five miles from Kanab Wash. Once there—assuming they could make it—they would face a whole new set of obstacles as they worked their way down the last hundred miles of the Grand Canyon. It had taken six hair-raising days through that section on the Major's first voyage. Since the Colorado was considerably higher and faster now, they could expect even more thrills. And there were more canyons beyond that. Even though Lieutenant Ives had mapped them fourteen years earlier on his upstream expedition, the Major wanted to see them firsthand and talked of following the Colorado all the way to the sea. The men were not so keen to continue the adventure quite that far.

On September 7—three days behind schedule—the boats finally pulled into Kanab Wash. Dutifully waiting, Adair and his helpers thought they were seeing ghosts. After fishing out Andy's coat, they were pretty sure the explorers had drowned, especially as other articles began floating by. It turned out that these were all items lost on August 31, when Powell's party left camp in a rush to escape the rising water.

Fresh supplies had a way of making past and future perils fade away like bad dreams. But along with the pack train of provisions brought by Adair was something the Major had not ordered, something that made the men wonder if they were destined to continue down the river after all. Nellie had taken it upon herself to send extra horses.

September 9, 1872

After breakfast around the campfire the Major leaned back in his chair, scratched his beard, cleared his throat, and announced, "Well, boys, our voyage is done." The men looked up. At first they were shocked, then disappointed, then immensely relieved. Powell went on to say that the reason was the high water and the risk of Indian attacks farther downstream, a possibility communicated to him by Adair based on rumors from a friendly Paiute. The Major had never let such threats stop him before. But most of the men didn't care why they were stopping. They wrote, essentially, "Hallelujah!" in their diaries and started to relax for the first time in months. But Clem thought he knew the real reason. Nellie had written him a note from Kanab implying that she was sending the horses as a message to her brother that enough was enough. There was no point in running the entire length of the canyon a second time. It was now time to mount up and leave before anyone was killed. The Major took the hint.

September–November 1872

The voyage might be over, but the expedition wasn't. The Major planned more trips to the region north of the Grand Canyon in order to complete his maps. His unshakable obsession meant that the Second Powell Expedition would not really end but would evolve into a permanent effort to study the geology and Indian cultures of the West. Powell had powerful supporters back in Washington, including his old commander at Shiloh and Vicksburg, General Grant, who was currently president of the United States. The frontier scientist from Illinois had found his life's work—and convinced the country's leaders to sponsor it.

Clem, however, wanted no more of it. He had decided that if he survived the Grand Canyon, he would be satisfied and head home at the first opportunity. The others were also ready to close this chapter of their lives—except for Prof, who would stay on as Powell's second-in-command, and Hillers, who was fascinated with his new career as the Major's photographer.

Even Fred was ready to end this unsurpassed adventure. He wrote to his parents: "I would come home right now but they don't consider the survey up until some land work is finished." That would take a few more months. The Major and Prof offered Fred the chance to stay on for four or five more years. But he declined. He was ready to go home, though he was certain that one way or another he would return to the West.

Fred's drawing of the Grand Canyon from the foot of the Toroweap Valley, November 1872. Ancient cascades of lava lie frozen in the middle distance. "What a conflict of water and fire there must have been here!" remarked the Major.

The Uinkaret Mountains, sketched by Fred near the spot where he made the drawing on page 103. The Grand Canyon can be glimpsed in the distance at the extreme left. A prominent volcanic cinder cone is in the center foreground. The leftmost peak of the major mountain range is named Mount Emma in honor of Mrs. Powell.

Throughout the fall the men explored mountains, deserts, buttes, extinct volcanoes, cliffs, canyons, creeks, and gullies in a series of adventures that would have been a lifetime supply for most people. At one point Fred and Jones found themselves on the north rim of the Grand Canyon looking down at a spot where the chasm was once plugged by lava flowing from a volcano sitting near the edge. Fred produced a sketch, which Jones called "the best he has made." The next day Fred made an equally expert drawing of the mountains and extinct volcanoes nearby. As an artist, he was coming into his own.

December 1872–February 1873

By Christmas, only Prof, Nellie, Hillers, and Fred were left. The Major had gone to Washington. Clem, Jones, and Andy had gone home.

Installed in a tent in Kanab, Fred was drawing the first map ever made of the Grand Canyon and the adjacent territory. By February 16, it was finished, and his last duty was to deliver it to the express office in Salt Lake City for shipment by train to the Major back east. Hillers, who had traveled to Salt Lake before, offered to guide Fred as far as the stagecoach line, about three days away by horseback.

On the second day out, Fred and Hillers reached a high summit in the middle of a blizzard.

"See any landmark?" asked Fred.

Mapping head-quarters in Kanab, Utah, January 1873. Fred is third from the left; next is Prof, then Nellie. The other two men are an assistant and a cook.

"Not a damned thing I ever saw before," replied Hillers.

They descended in what Hillers thought was the right direction until they reached an impasse. They backtracked. Fred had to fight his horse's desire to take a route that seemed wrong. Finally, they decided to let the animal have its way. After the storm cleared, the horse was proved correct. Another three days through snow and mud brought them to a stagecoach stop. But the line had been abandoned due to a horse epidemic. They kept riding. Fred could hardly see from snow blindness. By now they were in well-settled country where they could at least count on finding shelter each night, though one town had a sign warning them to stay away: SMALLPOX! They kept riding.

The ninth day brought them to a rail line where a Salt Lake–bound passenger train had gotten stalled in the drifts. Here, Fred and Hillers said their good-byes and parted. While the locomotive was being dug out, Fred climbed aboard with the map in one hand and his baggage in the other.

As he entered the train car, bright light from the snow-clad mountains flooded the old familiar interior. It gave him a strange feeling of both comfort and sadness, and he suddenly realized that for him the Second Powell Expedition was over. Late that afternoon he arrived in Salt Lake.

The express office had closed for the day, so Fred went looking for a hotel. He found the best one in town and was sitting in the lobby, dreamily contemplating sleep in a real room and a real bed for the first time in nearly two years, when he was approached by someone he knew. It was Bonnemort, the prospector who had waited with Captain Dodds at the Crossing of the Fathers sixteen months earlier, when the Second Powell Expedition seemed lost for sure. On that occasion Bonnemort had shown Fred how to pan for gold. Now he promised to make the young explorer a millionaire if he would join forces with him in the canyon country. Fred nodded absently as Bonnemort spun a tale of quick riches and a bright future. Sensing success, the prospector talked faster. But then he noticed Fred wasn't listening. "Think it over," he said gruffly, and left.

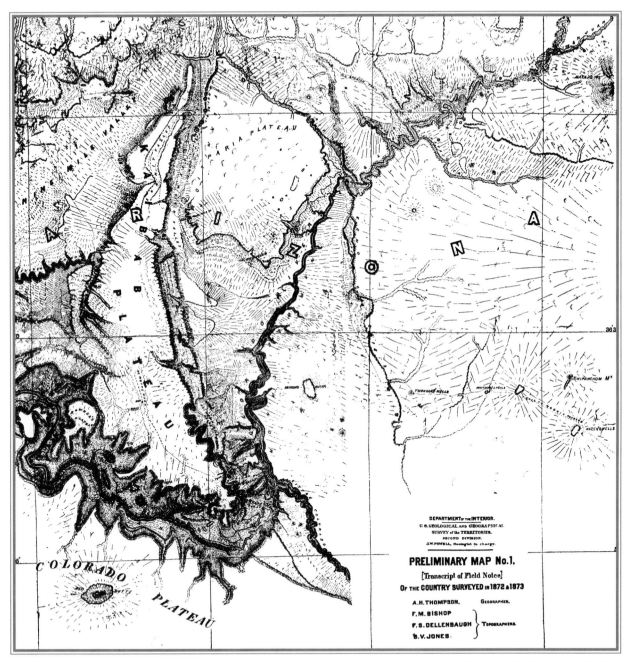

A published sheet prepared from the hand-drawn map of the Grand Canyon region completed by Fred in early 1873. The Colorado snakes from the top right corner to the center left edge, from just below the "mystery river" (the Escalante) to the point where the Major ended the voyage. Fred covered this distance between July 9 and September 7, 1872.

Fred's gaze followed him into the busy streets of the frontier city. It was true: Fred hadn't heard a thing. His thoughts were on a different kind of future. Envisioning the vast canvas of life stretched out before him, he could see a thousand different ways to fill it in. As always, Fred Dellenbaugh had a lot on his mind.

Fred, age nineteen, at the end of the Second Powell Expedition.

EPILOGUE
Farewell to the Wild Colorado

Fred arrived back in Buffalo on April 5, 1873, exactly two years to the day after he left. During the expedition the Major had done his best to turn his youngest recruit into a scientist-explorer. But Fred made up his mind to become an artist-explorer instead. In 1874, he left for Europe to do what all serious artists must: learn from the masters. The following year he returned to the Grand Canyon region to explore and paint, as he did often throughout his life. He also traveled to Alaska, Siberia, the Arctic, Iceland, Norway, the West Indies, and South America—always with pencils, brushes, sharp eyes, and a keen taste for adventure. Having learned respect for the Indians from the Major, he studied their ways and wrote a book, *The North Americans of Yesterday*. He wrote other books, including two on the Colorado, plus many stories and articles, all in a lively style with just enough of the "color" urged on him by the campfire critics of his early efforts during the Second Powell Expedition.

Strangely enough, the Second Powell Expedition was never mentioned in the official record. For reasons that puzzled Fred and angered the other men, the Major made it appear that events during the second expedition happened during the first. The result was a seamless, exciting story with all of the mishaps and uncertainties of the first trip combined with the wide-ranging explorations and scientific accomplishments of the second. But it was deceptive as history. The names of those on the first expedition became well known. Those on the second were not even recorded. Fred and his comrades found themselves in the unpleasant position of being judged liars for claiming to have voyaged down the Colorado with the Major.

In his letter to his sister from the Gates of Lodore, Fred implied that his drawings would appear together with Beaman's photographs and the Major's report. He certainly believed it. But it was not to be. Instead of being published, the drawings were filed away. The Major was not trying to be cruel. He was just busy. Amid his countless projects, his intentions to publish and interpret Fred's continuous sketch of the canyon walls never materialized. Powell went on to achieve great things. He helped start and lead the U.S. Geological Survey, he headed the Bureau of American Ethnology, and he tirelessly promoted sensible land use in the West and fair treatment for the Indians. But for some reason he never acknowledged the labors, risks, and accomplishments of the members of his second expedition down the Green and Colorado rivers.

Others in this story also achieved great things. Nellie became a leader in the crusade to secure voting rights for women, while Prof continued as the Major's loyal deputy, eventually serving as the chief geographer of the U.S. Geological Survey. Jones resumed his post as a school principal and studied law in his spare time. Later he moved to Dakota Territory and helped draft the state constitution for South Dakota. Steward returned to his former employer, a Chicago farm equipment manufacturer. There he worked so diligently that he was several times

offered raises. He always refused, insisting that the price of the equipment be reduced instead. Cap settled in Salt Lake City, becoming a Mormon, a college professor, and a mining entrepreneur. Andy returned to farming and finished his years at a disabled veterans' home, mixing war stories with wild tales of boating down the Colorado, which his fellow veterans doubtless didn't believe. Clem unfortunately died young about ten years after the expedition. At the time he was a druggist and civic leader in Omaha.

Almost nothing is known of Richardson except that he ended up back in Chicago. Beaman, too, disappeared into history, after photographing the region around the Grand Canyon on his own in 1872, and publishing his memoirs of the Powell trip in 1874.

Hillers, on the other hand, stayed with the Major for the rest of his career, making more than 20,000 superb pictures, which are considered some of the finest views of Western scenery and Indian life.

John D. Lee was finally captured by a U.S. marshal two years after Fred's visit to Lonely Dell. At his first trial, the jurors could not agree. At his second, they voted for conviction. In 1877, twenty years after the crime, the old man was led to the site of the Mountain Meadows massacre and executed by firing squad. He was the only person to be punished. Fennemore, long since recovered from his bout of ill health at Lonely Dell, was there to take the official picture.

In 1929, Fred went west for the last time. A few days short of his seventy-sixth birthday, he stopped in Salt Lake City for a reunion with Cap, now eighty-seven and the only other living member of the Second Powell Expedition. The two comrades reminisced, joked a bit, and posed for a newspaper photographer. Fred didn't stay long. Cap's poor health made it clear that soon Fred would be alone among the Major's men. Later in the trip he stopped in Kanab. The place had changed greatly in half a century, and few relics from the early days remained. One surprising survivor was a song that Fred had composed during the weeks of work on the map of the Grand Canyon. He and Hillers used to sing it in the evening when members of the community gathered for entertainment. It must have caught on, for some people were still singing it—though they were not quite sure what it was all about.

> *Oh, boys, you remember*
>   *The old Colorado,*
> *The* Nellie *and the* Dean
>   *And the* Cañonita, *too;*
> *The portages and "letdowns,"*
>   *The "blind box" and the "photos,"*
> *All flash through your minds*
>   *As do things of the past.*
>
> *Then farewell forever*
>   *To the wild Colorado;*
> *Its rapids and its rocks*
>   *Will trouble us no more;*
> *But we'll be free and merry,*
>   *Amidst old forms and faces,*
> *While the great foaming river*
>   *Dashes on to the sea.*

The Emma Dean *in Marble Canyon, August 1872.*

Author's Note

While writing this book, I knew it had to be illustrated with Fred Dellenbaugh's drawings, if at all possible. But I really held out very little hope that they still existed. I had never seen them published, and late in life Fred himself wrote that he had not seen them since they were shipped to Washington, D.C., in the course of the expedition. Imagine my surprise to find them one day listed on the Internet!—in the on-line catalog for the Smithsonian Institution. A trip down to Washington confirmed that, yes, these were Fred's originals, hundreds of them untouched for many decades. To my knowledge, these first drawings ever made of the Green and Colorado river canyons are published here for the first time.

As for Fred's story—until now, no one has told it in any detail except Fred himself. His 1908 memoir, *A Canyon Voyage*, follows the Second Powell Expedition from start to finish. I have drawn on it and on his earlier history, *The Romance of the Colorado River*, first published in 1902. I have also pored over Fred's Colorado River diary at the Rare Book and Manuscript Division of the New York Public Library, his photo collection at the Beinecke Library of Yale University, and, via mail, his letters and other papers relating to the trip at the University of Arizona Library and the Arizona Historical Society. In addition, I have read the diaries kept by every other expedition member (except Frank Richardson and Andy Hattan), most of which appeared in the *Utah Historical Quarterly*. I have researched the Beaman, Fennemore, and Hillers photographs at the National Archives, and I have consulted period newspapers, travel books, magazines, and other background material at the American Antiquarian Society in Worcester, Massachusetts, and Widener Library at Harvard University. I owe a deep debt of gratitude to each of these institutions.

In telling the story I have sometimes resorted to the methods of historical fiction to flesh out cases of skimpy data. One example is Fred's encounter with the couple on the train to Chicago in Chapter IV. I wanted to show Fred's state of mind and the attitudes of typical tourists of the day. Fred surely talked to such people, but I had to invent this particular couple to get the conversation going (which is why I didn't give them names). Fred's first meeting with the Major (also in Chapter IV) is based on a bit more information, but I still had to imagine the drift of the interview. The same goes for conversations relating to John D. Lee later in the book. The explorers actually lived with this notorious fugitive at his hideout, but left only intriguing clues about what was said. Footnotes would be out of place in a book like this; however, anyone wishing to follow my research trail should feel free to contact me in Holden, Massachusetts. One more warning: I have called territories, rivers, canyons, and other features by the names they were known at the time, so that, for example, the Grand River is no longer to be found on maps, having been reclassified as part of the Colorado.

A chance conversation with my wife's cousin Steven Amsterdam led me to a friend of his, Meg Dellenbaugh, who turned out to be Fred's great-granddaughter. She put me in touch with other members of her family, including her aunt Adele Dellenbaugh Hofmann, who as a young girl often played with her grandfather Fred. I was thrilled to talk to someone who actually knew the hero of my book, though I must admit it was disconcerting to hear about him as an old man just as I was getting to know him as a teenager. In important respects, however, he obviously had not changed—in kindness, nobility, sense of humor, and fascination with the West and its native inhabitants. These endured throughout his long life.

The late Austin Fox of the Nichols School in Buffalo, New York, gave me many leads for re-creating the thriving city of Fred's youth. William H. Loos of the Buffalo and Erie County Public Library also assisted me in this research. Jane Dutton and the late Jane A. Wilson of the Gale Free Library in Holden helped in many ways.

This book owes its existence to the constancy of my agent, Faith Hamlin, the enthusiasm of my editor, Simon Boughton, and the infinite indulgence of my family, Susie, Sam, and Joe.

—Richard Maurer

Suggested Reading

These are the most valuable published works I consulted, cited in their most recent editions. Some are hard to find, but all are well worth tracking down. Particularly recommended are Dellenbaugh's own account of the Second Powell Expedition, *A Canyon Voyage;* William H. Goetzmann's riveting survey of Western exploration in the 1800s, *Exploration and Empire;* and the intriguing photo book by Hal G. Stephens and Eugene M. Shoemaker, *In the Footsteps of John Wesley Powell.*

DIARIES AND MEMOIRS

E. O. Beaman, "The Cañon of the Colorado, and the Moquis Pueblos," *Appleton's Journal,* Vol. 11, 1874.

Francis Marion ("Cap") Bishop, "Captain Francis Marion Bishop's Journal," edited by Charles Kelly, *Utah Historical Quarterly,* Vol. 15, 1947.

Frederick S. Dellenbaugh (under pseudonym Justin Dale), "The Camp in the Gulch," *Oliver Optic's Magazine,* Vol. 15, 1874.

Frederick S. Dellenbaugh, *A Canyon Voyage: The Narrative of the Second Powell Expedition down the Green-Colorado River from Wyoming, and the Explorations on Land, in the Years 1871 and 1872* (University of Arizona Press, 1984).

Jack Hillers, *"Photographed All the Best Scenery": Jack Hillers' Diary of the Powell Expeditions, 1871–1875,* edited by Don D. Fowler (University of Utah Press, 1972).

Stephen Vandiver Jones, "Journal of Stephen Vandiver Jones," edited by Herbert E. Gregory, *Utah Historical Quarterly,* Vol. 16–17, 1948–49.

John D. Lee, *A Mormon Chronicle: The Diaries of John D. Lee,* edited by Robert Glass Cleland and Juanita Brooks (University of Utah Press, 1983).

John Wesley Powell, *The Exploration of the Colorado River and Its Canyons* (Penguin USA, 1997). Formerly titled: *Canyons of the Colorado.*

John Wesley Powell, "John Wesley Powell's Journal: Colorado River Exploration 1871–1872," edited by Don D. Fowler and Catherine S. Fowler, *The Smithsonian Journal of History,* Vol. 3, No. 2, Summer 1968.

Walter Clement ("Clem") Powell, "Journal of W. C. Powell," edited by Charles Kelly, *Utah Historical Quarterly,* Vol. 16–17, 1948–49.

John F. Steward, "Journal of John F. Steward," edited by William Culp Darrah, *Utah Historical Quarterly*, Vol. 16–17, 1948–49.

Almon Harris ("Prof") Thompson, "Diary of Almon Harris Thompson," edited by J. Cecil Alter, *Utah Historical Quarterly*, Vol. 7, 1939.

Ellen Powell ("Nellie") Thompson, "The 1872 Diary and Plant Collections of Ellen Powell Thompson," edited by Beatrice Scheer Smith, *Utah Historical Quarterly*, Vol. 62, Spring 1994.

HISTORIES, BIOGRAPHIES, ETC.

Juanita Brooks, *The Mountain Meadows Massacre* (University of Oklahoma Press, 1991).

Fred A. Conetah, *A History of the Northern Ute People,* edited by Kathryn L. MacKay and Floyd A. O'Neil (Uintah-Ouray Ute Tribe, 1982).

William Culp Darrah, *Powell of the Colorado* (Princeton University Press, 1951).

Frederick S. Dellenbaugh, *The Romance of the Colorado River: The Story of Its Discovery in 1540, with an Account of the Later Explorations, and with Special Reference to the Voyages of Powell Through the Line of the Great Canyons* (Time-Life Books, 1982).

William H. Goetzmann, *Exploration and Empire: The Explorer and the Scientist in the Winning of the American West* (Texas State Historical Association, 1994).

Gary C. Nichols, *River Runners' Guide to Utah and Adjacent Areas* (University of Utah Press, 1986).

Frederick E. Shearer, editor, *The Pacific Tourist: J. R. Bowman's Illustrated Trans-Continental Guide of Travel from the Atlantic to the Pacific Ocean* (J. R. Bowman, Publisher, 1882–83).

Wallace Stegner, *Beyond the Hundredth Meridian: John Wesley Powell and the Second Opening of the West* (Penguin USA, 1992).

Hal G. Stephens and Eugene M. Shoemaker, *In the Footsteps of John Wesley Powell: An Album of Comparative Photographs of the Green and Colorado Rivers, 1871–72 and 1968* (Johnson Books, 1987).

Doug Wheat, *The Floater's Guide to Colorado* (Falcon Press Publishing Company, 1983).

Index

Page numbers in *italics* refer to illustrations and maps

Picture Credits

Pages **2, 6, 8** Yale Collection of Western Americana, Beinecke Rare Book and Manuscript Library; **11** Joseph C. Ives, *Report upon the Colorado River of the West* (Government Printing Office, 1861); **12** Samuel Bowles, *Across the Continent* (S. Bowles and Co., 1869); **17, 21** John Wesley Powell, *The Exploration of the Colorado River and Its Canyons* (Dover Publications, 1961); **25** Yale Collection of Western Americana, Beinecke Rare Book and Manuscript Library; **27** courtesy Harvard Map Collection; **30** National Anthropological Archives, Smithsonian Institution; **33, 36-37, 38** Yale Collection of Western Americana, Beinecke Rare Book and Manuscript Library; **41** Kayley LeFaiver; **45** National Archives; **46** (top) National Archives; (bottom) National Anthropological Archives, Smithsonian Institution; (left) Frederick S. Dellenbaugh, *The Romance of the Colorado River* (G.P. Putnam's Sons, 1902); **48** National Archives; **52, 54-55** National Anthropological Archives, Smithsonian Institution; **57** Dellenbaugh Collection number 43219, courtesy of the Arizona Historical Society/Tucson; **58** Yale Collection of Western Americana, Beinecke Rare Book and Manuscript Library; **60-61** (drawing) National Anthropological Archives, Smithsonian Institution; **61** (photo) National Archives; **62, 64-65, 67, 68** National Anthropological Archives, Smithsonian Institution; **69** (left) Yale Collection of Western Americana, Beinecke Rare Book and Manuscript Library; (right) National Archives; **72** John D. Lee, *Mormonism Unveiled* (Sun Publishing Co., 1882); **77, 80** National Archives; **85** (top) Thomas B. H. Stenhouse, *The Rocky Mountain Saints* (D. Appleton and Co., 1873); (bottom) John D. Lee, *Mormonism Unveiled* (Sun Publishing Co., 1882); **90** National Archives; **91** National Anthropological Archives, Smithsonian Institution; **94-95, 98** National Archives; **103, 104-105** National Anthropological Archives, Smithsonian Institution; **105** (bottom) Dellenbaugh Collection number 43215, courtesy of the Arizona Historical Society/Tucson; **107** Frederick S. Dellenbaugh, *A Canyon Voyage* (G.P. Putnam's Sons, 1908); **108, 110, 111** (left) Yale Collection of Western Americana, Beinecke Rare Book and Manuscript Library; **111** (right) *Salt Lake Tribune*; **113** National Archives.